Earth Water Fire Air

A Waldorf Songbook

"Earth, water, fire and air,
Weave the body that you bear,
The elements four each have their share..."

Earth Water Fire Air

A Waldorf Songbook

Peter Patterson

Wynstones Press

Published by
Wynstones Press
Stourbridge
England.

www.wynstonespress.com

First edition 2014

Cover design by Christiana Bryan, aged 15.
Headline typeface: Sagittar, designed by Christiana Bryan.

Printed in EU.

ISBN 9780 946206 292

My Pigeon House	9	Poetic Edda	46
Mother of the Fairy Tale	10	Sigurd and the Dragon	48
Golden Sun, Arise	11	Snow White: round	49
Little Mary Winecups	12	Celtic Blessing	50
Good Angel	14	The Lord of Falkenstein	51
The Heavens Above	15	Kalevala the chant lines	52
The Lady Moon	16	Kalevala accompaniment	53
The Water of Life	17	Kalevala interlude	54
The Sun is in my Heart	18	Now the day has come	55
Easy Questions	19	The Golden Time: canon	56
King Mansolain	20	The Golden Time bass part	57
King Mansolain 2	21	Coffee Song	58
King Mansolain 3	22	Flying Song	59
The King of the Copper Mountains	23	Acrobat: round	60
Granny's Wonderful Chair	24	Joyous is the Day	61
Painting Song	25	Pretty Colours	62
The King of Ireland's Son 1	26	Old Tom's Songbadil	63
The King of Ireland's Son 2	27	Song of the Nature Spirits	64
The King of Ireland's Son 3	28	Song of the Nature Spirits 2	65
The King of Ireland's Son 4	31	Song of the Nature Spirits 3	66
Number Song	32	Song of the Nature Spirits 4	67
Ring Dance for the Lord	34	Birds: round	68
Ring Dance 2	36	Hymn to the Dawn	70
Solomon's Temple	38	Vedic chant – to Vishnu	72
Raphael	39	Gayatri Mantra	74
I Greet the Day	40	Egyptian Dance	75
Of All Created Things	41	Hymn to U-si-re	78
Odin, the Wanderer	42	Gilgamesh	79
Music for a Norse Play 1	43	Searching Satyrs 1	80
Norse Play 2	44	Searching Satyrs 3	81

Searching Satyrs 2 — 82
Roman Music 1 — 84
Roman Song — 85
Ancient Greek Dance — 86
Birds are Winging — 87
Sadness and Mirth — 88
All is Silent — 89
The Lord, We Say: canon — 90
Merry Let Us Be: round — 91
Swallows — 92
The Elven Halleluia — 93
Michael, the Victorious — 94
Michael Song 2 — 95
Michael Song 3 — 96
Table Blessing Alleluia — 97
The Song of the Road — 98
Rhythm Round — 100
Bulgarian Dance Rhythms — 101
Exaltate — 104
Funky Greeting — 105
Gelmindel — 106
Gloria Deo — 109
Music from West Africa — 110
West Africa 2: Evua, the Sun God — 112
Joyous Alleluia — 114
Joyous Alleluia accompaniments — 115
Mystic Alleluia — 116
Splendid Alleluia — 117
Antigone chorus 1 — 118
Antigone chorus 2 — 120

Antigone chorus 3 — 121
Antigone chorus 4 — 124
Antigone chorus 5 — 126
Antigone chorus 6: final — 127
Antigone chorus 6 percussion — 129
Midsummer Music: round — 130
Winter: round — 131
The Forest Folk: round — 132
Koko, the Clown: canon — 133
Magic Bee Song — 134
Beethoven's Impatience — 136
Climbing Up — 138
Peace Song — 139
Salve Regina 1 — 140
Salve Regina 2 — 141
Seasons — 142
Shadow World — 143
Dragon Dances, for baby and mature dragons — 146
Dragon Dances, for elegant dragons — 148
Summer's End — 151
The Birch Tree and the Wild Rose — 152
The Chevy Chase — 156
Fiddle Dance — 160
The Rainbow — 162
Yr Hen Wr Mwyn – The Kind Old Man — 166

The items in this book arose while I was teaching in various Waldorf schools over a period of more than fifty years, in Germany, England and New Zealand. I have arranged them in an appropriate order with regard to the age of the young people singing them, though I don't very much like rules about when a song is or is not suitable. You might feel that earlier or later is different with the various classes you teach, and singing to your own children at home might be different again.

Waldorf teachers usually find that up to around the age of seven, 'pentatonic' songs are beneficial. This means the tunes use a 5-note scale, usually the Chinese pentatonic that is favoured in Waldorf kindergartens. Old Scottish folk music uses a similar scale. There are other pentatonic scales in the world, for instance the two beautiful Balinese scales, called 'slendro' and 'pelog', with the intervals arranged quite differently from the Chinese/Scottish/Waldorf scale of D E G A B. And, incidentally, this latter scale can be sung at different pitches, to suit the range of the singers. So for instance, C D F G A is exactly the same scale, just one tone lower. Choose the pitch to suit the range of the voices you have.

I see nothing sacrosanct about having D as the lowest note. The peculiarity of the Chinese pentatonic scale is that it has 'no feet', any note can be felt as the final, the scale 'floats in the air' and does not therefore induce the pre-school and kindergarten child to come down to earth too soon. And please don't confuse 'pentatonic' with Rudolf Steiner's idea of music "in the mood of the fifth", which he recommends for the youngest classes. The mood of the fifth is a quite different principle. Steiner was a child in an environment greatly influenced by Hungarian folk culture and will have heard folk music that is typically within the span of a fifth. Tunes in old Hungarian folk music can sometimes get away with using only three or four notes, or they might use a grouping like C D E F G, with often a note above and below as a momentary extension of the range, but basically using the notes within the range of the fifth. In other words, keeping to the mood of the fifth even though here and there a note or two outside the frame might occur, making six or seven notes actually in use. And at the other extreme we can easily devise pentatonic songs that have a far greater range than the fifth and have nothing whatsoever to do with the "mood of the fifth" but are still pentatonic. If you're as old as me you might remember Paul Robeson's famous "Old Man River", a gorgeous pentatonic song with a range of more that an octave and certainly not in the mood of the fifth or suitable for the kindergarten! The Waldorf principle is not to stretch, as it were, the young child's life energies, what we call the "etheric body", by singing songs with too great a range too soon. And here we need to make a very clear distinction between singing and listening. It can be very beneficial for the very young child, for instance, even when only days or weeks old, to have you gently play a circle of fifths while she or he is going to sleep, say on a lyre. A circle of fifths means for example C G D above the G, A above that, and slowly down again. I once knew a very poorly baby that had the most dreadful and incurable sleeping problems. He just cried and cried for hours, nothing would console him. And the poor parents! When I played a circle of fifths slowly on a lyre, the baby was instantly and permanently cured of his disharmony and had a healthy sleep ever after! Of course it would be absurd to try to get a child to sing fifths in this way. That would be against the natural development of the child and would constitute a grotesque misunderstanding of the idea of the mood of the fifth. Our pentatonic songs for the kindergarten and Class One need to be chosen with this distinction between singing and listening to an instrument very clearly and responsibly in mind.

As the children get older, both classes and individual children are never uniformly plain sailing or predictable, and whatever the problems or the gifts, music can be a great help. From Rudolf Steiner's teaching, we have basic guidelines for understanding the development of the child. But we must avoid standardisation and dogma. For example, some classes are relatively slow in their development and would find the challenge of singing rounds in Class Three stressful, in which case they should usually not be forced but allowed to wait a while. Other classes will embrace the singing of rounds in Class Three with ease and joy. Encourage them, but best not push if they don't enjoy the challenge. Later we might find it necessary and beneficial to give them a push into new territory. For example, my settings of the choruses from the "Antigone" by Sophocles were written originally for another teacher's Class Eight. When I introduced the music to them they found it totally weird and said they would never be able to sing the unfamiliar scales and rhythms. After a week I heard the students sing the melodies in the playground with enthusiasm. In the performances, audiences said they were 'blown away' by the exciting sounds.

In the remarks attached to the songs I have sometimes made recommendations as to when the music might be appropriate. But do remember nothing is intended to be prescriptive. As a parent or teacher bring in your own sensitivity and insight as a guide as well as the principles of the curriculum.

Some of my most successful songs have been my settings of poems by Tolkien. For copyright reasons these cannot be printed with the lyrics. Nevertheless I have included just a few in this collection, the most loved ones, without the texts, but indicating where you can find the words that would fit.

Peter Patterson, 2014

My Pigeon House

Peter Patterson

My pi - geon house I o - pen wide and set all my pi - geons free. They

fly a - round on ev - 'ry side up to the high - est tree. Then

they come back at e - ven - tide and close their eyes and sing:

Croo - coo, croo - coo, croo - coo.

2. Tomorrow they'll all fly away
   to visit the hills and dales.
   They'll fly and fly both far and wide
   until the daylight fails.
   Then they'll come back at eventide
   and close their eyes and sing:
   Croo-coo, croo-coo, croo-coo.

Mother of the Fairy Tale

Peter Patterson

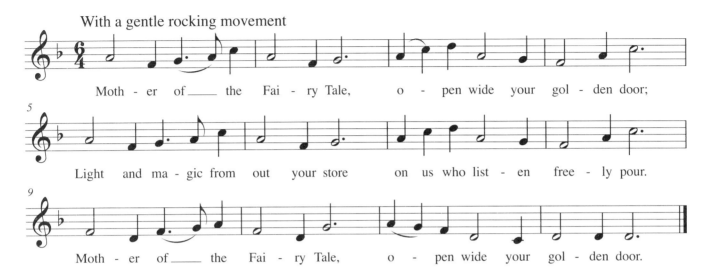

With a gentle rocking movement

Moth - er of —— the Fai - ry Tale, o - pen wide your gol - den door;

Light and ma - gic from out your store on us who list - en free - ly pour.

Moth - er of —— the Fai - ry Tale, o - pen wide your gol - den door.

2. Mother of the Fairy Tale,
   take us to your shining land;
   sail us in your silver boat,
   sail us silently afloat.
   Mother of the Fairy Tale,
   take us to your shining land.

This song is especially for the younger children, to be sung by them when they are ready
to hear the story. A triangle and some gentle bells could join in the background.

Golden Sun, Arise

Peter Patterson

Gol - den sun, a - rise,_____ to you I lift my eyes;_____ with long - ing and with joy I wait to see__ you pass__ the mor - ning gate._____

2. Golden sun, now glow,
   oh, leave me not alone,
   and chase away all cloud and cold,
   your heavenly word to me unfold.

This is for the younger children.

Little Mary Winecups

Peter Patterson

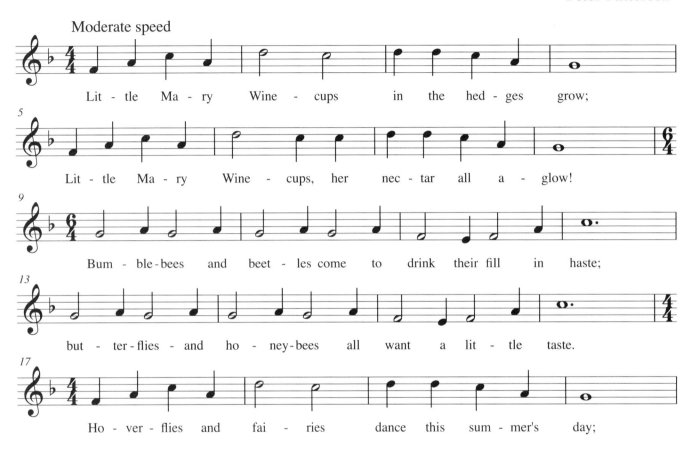

Lit - tle Ma - ry Wine - cups in the hed - ges grow;

Lit - tle Ma - ry Wine - cups, her nec - tar all a - glow!

Bum - ble-bees and beet - les come to drink their fill in haste;

but - ter-flies - and ho - ney-bees all want a lit - tle taste.

Ho - ver - flies and fai - ries dance this sum - mer's day;

Lit - tle Ma - ry Wine - cups gives the gold a - way.

Frogs and toads in won - der smile and stare at what they see;

bum - ble-bees and fai - ries come and want to play with me.

Lit - tle Ma - ry Wine - cups in the hed - ges grow;

Lit - tle Ma - ry Wine - cups, her nec - tar all a - glow!

This song is for the younger children, especially those of Class One. It can be accompanied by triangles and small cymbals played gently in the background, mostly just once a bar.

Good Angel

Peter Patterson

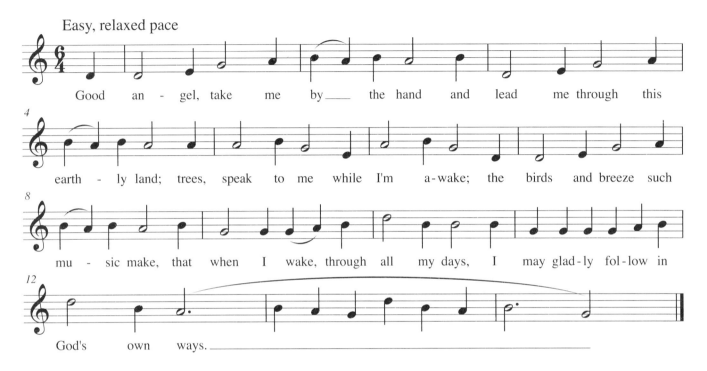

Good an - gel, take me by the hand and lead me through this earth - ly land; trees, speak to me while I'm a-wake; the birds and breeze such mu - sic make, that when I wake, through all my days, I may glad-ly fol-low in God's own ways.

2. At night, good angel, be my guide
   that I among the stars abide;
   stars, speak to me while I'm asleep,
   your loving watch forever keep,
   that when I wake, through all my days,
   I may gladly follow in God's own ways.

This song was written to follow the morning verse of the younger primary classes.

The Heavens Above

Peter Patterson

With a joyful swing

The heav'ns a-bove and the earth be-low, and an-gels fly-ing to_____ and fro, and on the earth so firm I stand, I stretch out my hand to greet____ my friend._____

2. In smile of human, song of bird,
   I treasure all I've seen or heard;
   I open wide my heart today
   through eyes and ears, in work and play.

3. Each morning when from dreams I wake
   my angel says: "Life's journey take!
   A kind word always give to all,
   whoever shall for friendship call!"

4. With joy we'll greet then all we see,
   in friend and beast, in flower and tree,
   in rain and rainbow, moon and sun,
   until we sleep when day is done.

5. The heavens above and the earth below,
   in God's own image I will grow;
   my angel, walking by my side,
   will help wherever I abide.

Some classes may find it more comfortable to sing this morning song a tone or even a third lower.
Be like J. S. Bach, who never hesitated to transpose a piece into a different key, so that the pitch could
suit the instruments or voices!

The Lady Moon

Peter Patterson

With a gentle rocking movement

The La - dy Moon up yon - der is like a sil - ver boat _____ up -
on a dark blue o - cean, all si - lent - ly a - float. _____
Oh, take me on a voy - age be -
yond and through the night. _____ to where the stars are shi - ning in
lands so fair and bright. _____ The La - dy Moon up
yon - der, she whis - pers in my heart: _____ "My sil - ver boat un -
furls her sail, be rea - dy to de - part. _____

The Water of Life

Peter Patterson

This song is for Class One but can be sung anywhere you think appropriate.

The Sun is in my Heart

Peter Patterson

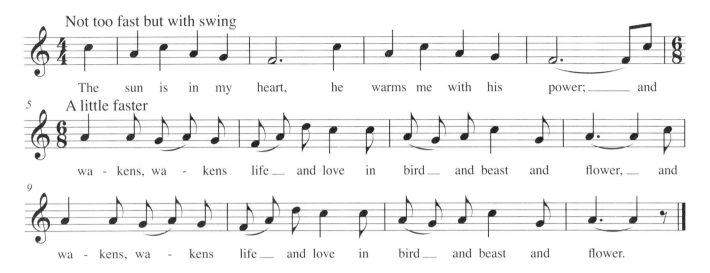

2. The stars above my head
   are shining in my mind
   as spirits, spirits of the world
   that in my thoughts I find....

3. The earth whereon I tread
   lets not my feet go through
   but strongly, strongly does uphold
   the weight of deeds I do....

4. Then must I thankful be
   that here on earth I dwell,
   to know, to know and love the world
   and work all creatures well....

Text by Cecil Harwood, edited.

18

Easy Questions

Peter Patterson

2. And who's that wee man we see, riding by himself?
Furry feet and curly hair, neither dwarf nor elf!
Strange little fellow there, dwarf's cloak and curly hair!

3. Can you guess the wizard's name, riding as their aid?
And that one who also came, hobbit unafraid?
Strange little fellow there, dwarf's cloak and curly hair!

King Mansolain

Peter Patterson

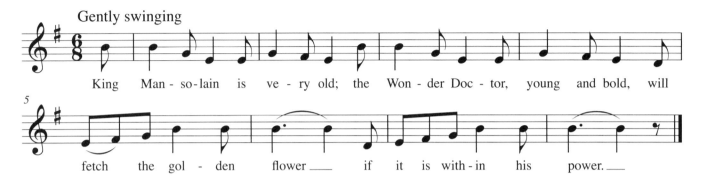

Gently swinging

King Man - so-lain is ve - ry old; the Won - der Doc - tor, young and bold, will

fetch the gol - den flower ___ if it is with - in his power. ___

2. King Mansolain and his faithful hare! His beard is long and his halls are bare,
   but animals come to share and show just how much they care.

For later in the story:
3. Fierce wolf and dragon, duck and sheep, the beetle and squirrel, up they leap.
   The King is so very pale, so each tells a special tale.

4. The woods are green, the sea is blue, bleeze-bleezy, baa-baa, quack-quack, coo.
   The castle is red and gold; the snow is so very cold.

5. We all sing queekle, baa-baa, boom, we sing to the King in the copper room;
   we sing to King Mansolain to make him feel well again.

This much loved little song is to be sung by the class before each story session from "The King of the Copper Mountains", by Paul Biegel (Class One or Two). You can make up other verses as the stories progress.

King Mansolain 2

Peter Patterson

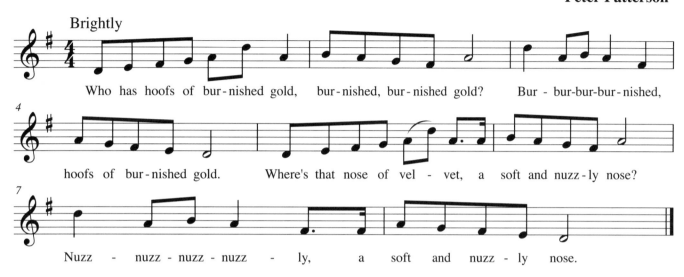

Brightly

Who has hoofs of bur-nished gold, bur-nished, bur-nished gold? Bur - bur-bur-bur-nished,

hoofs of bur-nished gold. Where's that nose of vel - vet, a soft and nuzz-ly nose?

Nuzz - nuzz-nuzz-nuzz - ly, a soft and nuzz - ly nose.

This song goes with the Horse's story. Try making up verses with the children for other stories, then make up a simple tune. The children will help you.

King Mansolain 3

Peter Patterson

Everyone cries "Done! Done!" at the end. It is nice to add a triangle and one other gentle percussion instrument to this song.

Another example of how you can make up a simple song, easy in this case because the two mice are adorably simple people. Their silly song could be sung as a round.

The King of the Copper Mountains

Peter Patterson

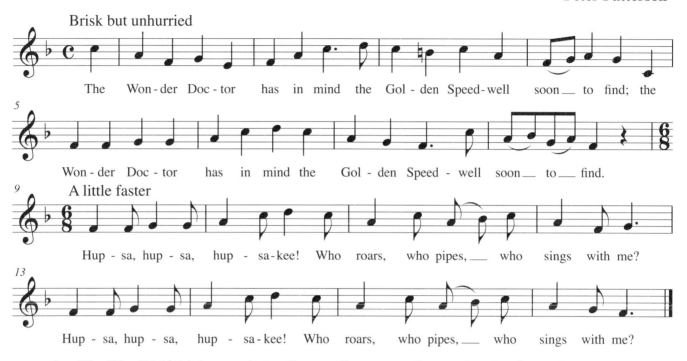

2. The Woe Wolf thinks no witches live, until strange calls an echo give (repeat).
   Hupsa, hupsa, hupsakee! Who roars, who pipes, who sings with me? (repeat).
3. Giraffe and squirrel, with bushy tail; that squirrel's smart, his plan won't fail. Hupsa...
4. The Rabbit-of -the-dunes is sad; but what has happened is not bad. Hupsa...
5. A tiny dwarf must cross a pond, of wishing-flowers he's very fond. Hupsa...
6. Miskindir, gentle dog so strong, protects the sheep from any wrong. Hupsa...
7. A beetle and a cherry tree; the spider says, "Don't bother me!" Hupsa...
8. A lion, a witch who ruins time! The prince says what she did's a crime. Hupsa...
9. A mighty cliff is such a block; the Doctor cannot climb the rock. Hupsa...
10. There comes the Horse with hoofs of gold; the Wonder Doctor is so cold. Hupsa...
11. The Dragon with three heads bows low; he brings a tale from long ago. Hupsa...
12. The Mice sing also their own tune, then "Done!" they cry; it's bed-time soon. Hupsa...
13. The wizard's child invites her friends; the party with her weeping ends. Hupsa...
14. The two black lakes, the freezing cold; the snow will hide the Speedwell's gold. Hupsa...
15. The Donkey has his tale to tell; the King is sad at what befell. Hupsa...
16. Then comes the greatest tale of all, when dwarfs were small, the young King tall. Hupsa...
17. The Doctor brings the magic flower; it saves the King with healing power. Hupsa...

23

Granny's Wonderful Chair

Peter Patterson

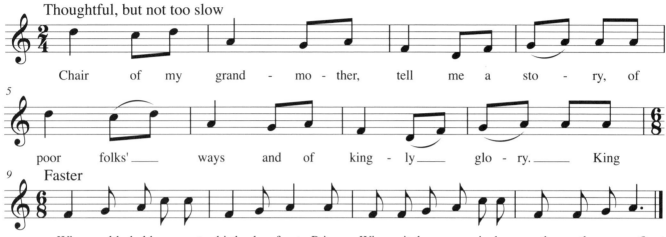

Thoughtful, but not too slow

Chair of my grand - mo - ther, tell me a sto - ry, of

poor folks' _____ ways and of king - ly _____ glo - ry. _____ King

Faster

Win - wealth held a great birth - day feast; Prince Wise - wit has gone, is he north, south, or east?

2. Wantall and Greedalind, queen and princess are they,
   spiteful and selfish, they have nothing kind to say.
   King Winwealth held a great birthday feast;
   Prince Wisewit has gone, is he north, south, or east?

3. Wondrous the tales that are told from her granny's chair
   when Snowflower rests her fair head on the cushion there.
   King Winwealth held a great birthday feast;
   Prince Wisewit has gone, is he north, south, or east?

"Granny's Wonderful Chair" by the young blind woman, Frances Browne, is one of the most treasured collections of stories for Class 2, though older children will love them just as much. The children can sing this song at the beginning of every day's story time. Get them to make up more verses for each of the separate stories. Get them to act episodes out of the stories, too.

Painting Song

Peter Patterson

Unhurried

Rain - bow, rain - bow, love - ly glow, put some co - lour in my hand, to - geth - er we'll make _ a ma - gic land. _____ Through the rain - bow, there I'll find hun - dreds of col - ours in my mind. So if you'll_ hush_ I'll use my brush for you!_____

This song is for singing at the beginning of the painting lesson when everything is completely ready to begin putting colour on the paper. And hush! Do you all think now we can work in silence?

The King of Ireland's Son I

Peter Patterson

This is the poem in the book. Get the children to make up more verses as the story goes along.

The wonderful story of The King of Ireland's Son by Padraic Colum is published by Floris Books, Edinburgh. This story is often told to the children of Class 2 in Waldorf Schools, and we are grateful to Floris Books for their kind permission to reproduce the words of the four songs published here.

The King of Ireland's Son 2

Peter Patterson

Again, these are the words in the book, but verses can be added as part of the students' creative response to the story.

The King of Ireland's Son 3

Peter Patterson

1. The black-bird shakes ___ his me-tal notes a-gainst the edge ___ of day, ___ and I ___ am left up-on ___ my road with one star on my way. 2. The night has told ___ it to the hills and told the

par - tridge in the nest ____ and left ____ it on the

long ____ white roads, she will give light in - stead of rest. 3. Be -

hold the sky is cov - ered as with a migh - ty shroud: ____ a

for - lorn light is ly - ing be - tween the earth and

Continued over....

cloud.   4. In the si - lence of the mor - ning my - self,

my - self went by, _____ where lone - ly trees sway

bran - ches and leaves   a - gainst __ spa - ces of the sky

Unless the children are well advanced in music this song is likely to be too difficult for Class 2.
But if the class does a play of the King of Ireland's son, the teacher might arrange for an older class to
perform it with the actors. It gives the children quite a boost when classes work together in this way.

The King of Ireland's Son 4

Peter Patterson

Merrily

A ber - ry, a ber - ry, a red ro - wan ber - ry, a red __ ro - wan ber - ry

brought me beau - ty and love. But drops of my heart's __ blood, drops of my heart's __ blood,

se - ven drops of my heart's blood I have gi - ven a - way. Se - ven wild __ geese were men,

se - ven wild __ geese were men, se - ven drops of my __ heart's blood are there for your spell. A

kiss for my true __ love, a kiss for my true __ love, may his kiss __ go __ to none

till we meet __ a - gain. If to some - one go his kiss, if to some - one go his kiss,

he __ may __ meet me a - gain and ne - ver know __ me more.

Number Song

Peter Patterson

we now all go out to dine? Eight eights are migh - ty six - ty four and

nine nines are eigh - ty one. And so our song___ is near - ly done for

ten tens are one less than one oh one. Now we're all tired, our

fa - ces are red, for we have reached one hun - der - ed!

What is the "magic N"? If you make a circle of ten digits, zero to nine, with zero at the top and five at the bottom, try connecting up the digits according to the table of numbers multiplied by themselves, the numbers in this song. So you connect one to four, four to nine, nine to six (of the 'sixteen'), six to five (of the 'twenty-five'), five back to six ('36'), six back to nine, nine to four, four to one, and one to zero (for the 100). And there is a strange sort of N, the "magic N" of the song.

Ring Dance for the Lord

Peter Patterson

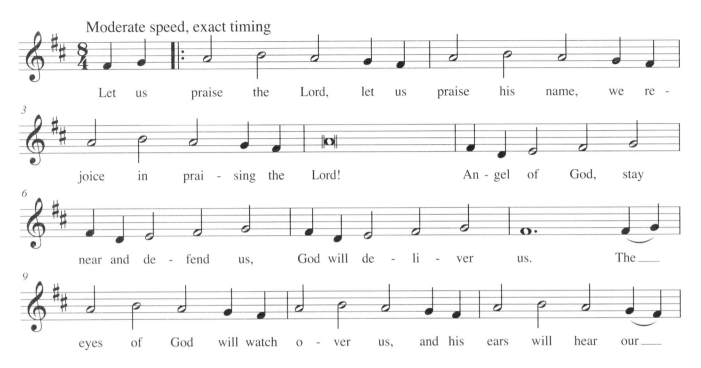

Moderate speed, exact timing

Let us praise the Lord, let us praise his name, we re -
joice in prai - sing the Lord! An - gel of God, stay
near and de - fend us, God will de - li - ver us. The___
eyes of God will watch o - ver us, and his ears will hear our___

34

prayer. An - gel of God, stay near and de - fend us,

God will de - li - ver us. Let us

Drum rhythms, untuned

In Class 3 of the Waldorf Schools we traditionally study many of the wonderful stories from the Old Testament, or Torah. This simple song is a ring dance that the children will enjoy. The student or students providing the percussion should follow the 4-bar unit above for untuned hand-drums. Ignore the treble clef! They should be encouraged to play very steadily, exactly in time, without hurrying any beats. Stop at the end of any section.

Ring Dance 2

Peter Patterson

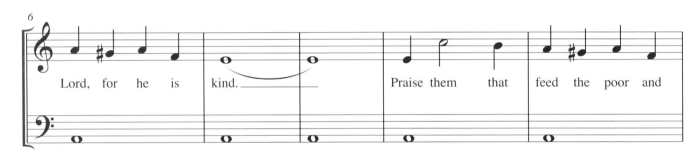

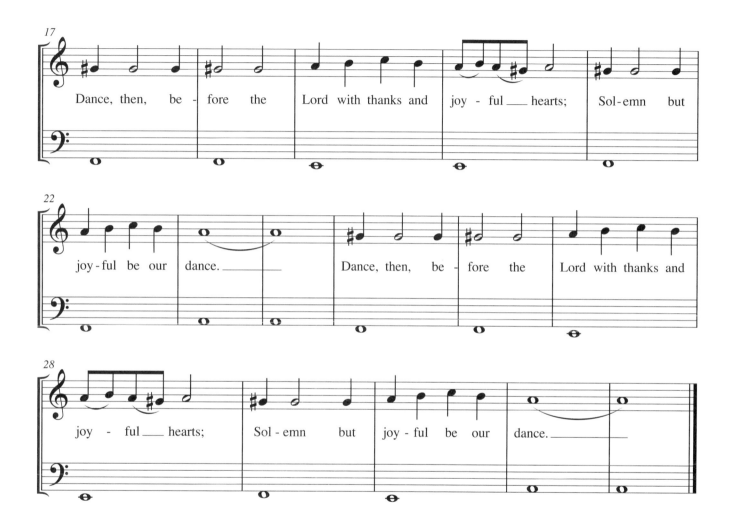

This again is an energetic ring dance for Class 3, in the context of their Torah or Old Testament studies. Ideally, use a harp of some sort for the deep bass notes, otherwise the piano or lowest guitar strings, or whatever you have.

Make up further verses out of whatever stories the children are busy with.

Solomon's Temple

Peter Patterson

Rather slow but not dragging

We strive the tem-ple to build for the Lord, with ce - dar, sil - ver and gold. _____ Its

migh - ty pil - lars the roof ___ will raise, the Ark here to ___ en - fold. _____

2. Behold the pillars we put here in place
   these arches to support;
   the Temple ever shall witness our faith,
   our fervent prayers escort.

3. God's holy Ark we carry within
   between the seraphs so bright;
   the Lord has given the Ark his strength,
   His presence shines with light.

You will have noticed that while the Cs are sharp, the Fs are not - an unusual scale. I try to expand the children's hearing beyond the everyday major and minor scales, and a good time to begin doing that is Class 3, when they are immersed in the stories of the Old Testament or Jewish Torah, taking them into faraway times and a world of sights and sounds different from what they are likely to know.

The song is a slow processional, the children coming to stand in pairs as pillars, holding out their arms to one another to form the roof beams, miming the building of the Temple, bringing the Ark into it, and so on.

Raphael

A three-part round

Peter Patterson

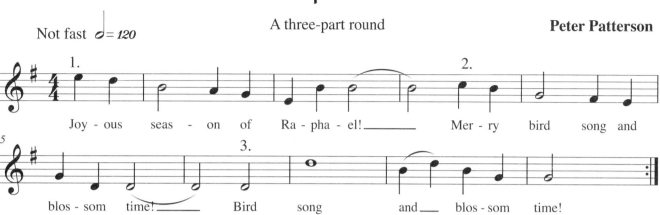

Joy - ous   seas - on   of   Ra - pha - el!_____   Mer - ry   bird   song   and

blos - som   time!_____   Bird   song   and__ blos - som   time!

I Greet the Day

Peter Patterson

With a cheerful swing

Optional chords:

I greet the day, the new - born day, with all it holds___ in store:_____ its joys and sor - rows, yet___ un-known, my soul wants to ex - plore._____

2. Sleep took me to the world of stars
   their strength lives now in me.
   within the newborn world of day
   I want to grow and be.

3. The wonders that surround me yield
   their secrets to my will
   when I in reverence learn to use
   my senses and my skill.

4. As the fair sun illuminates
   the day for me with light,
   my soul that wants to do the good
   shall be my inner guide.

5. In heart and sun, in stars of night,
   the power of God holds sway;
   with Him and through Him I will grow
   into the newborn day.

(Words by Hans van der Stok)

Of All Created Things

Brisk and energetic

Peter Patterson

Optional chords:

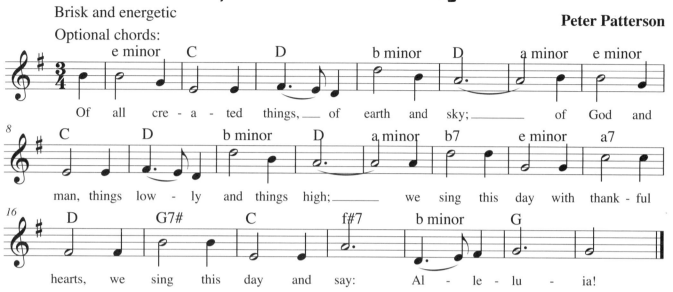

2. Of sun and moon, the lamps of night and day,
   stars and the planets, sounding on their way;
   we sing this day.... etc....

3. Of times and seasons, evening and fresh morn,
   of birth and death, green blade and golden corn;
   we sing this day....

4. Of all that lives and moves, the winds a-blow,
   fire, and old ocean's never resting flow;
   we sing this day....

5. Of earth, and from earth's darkness springing free,
   the flowers outspread, the heavenward reaching tree;
   we sing this day....

6. My human hand outstretched for service high,
   courage at heart, truth in my steadfast eye;
   we sing this day....

This is a popular morning song, with words by the late Cecil Harwood. I have edited them just a little.

Odin, the Wanderer

Peter Patterson

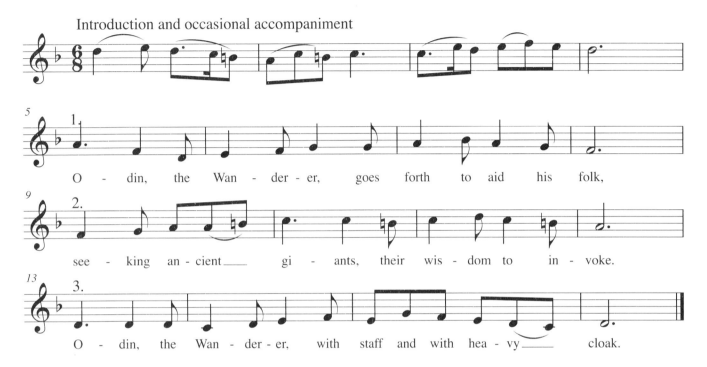

Introduction and occasional accompaniment

1. O - din, the Wan - der - er, goes forth to aid his folk,

2. see - king an - cient___ gi - ants, their wis - dom to in - voke.

3. O - din, the Wan - der - er, with staff and with hea - vy___ cloak.

2. Gungnir's his mighty spear, his ravens are famous, too;
   Far and wide they fly for him more knowledge to accrue;
   Huginn and Muninn fly up into the sky's deep blue.

3. Fire could not damage him, and when he hung on the Tree
   Dying brought new life to him, his mind grew strong and free.
   Odin, the wisdom seeker, striving eternally.

This piece was written for Class 4, a year when we like to learn about the mythologies of northern Europe. Sing as a round or just a song in plain unison. The first four bars can be played on the pipe or other instrument as both an introduction and as an accompaniment whenever needed.

Music for a Norse Play I

Peter Patterson

This is the song of the Giants from the Class 4 play about Thor and Loki visiting the Giants to get Thor's hammer back. This is only the first verse in the play, sung of course by the Giants, who are very impressive walking around on hidden stilts. You can make up other verses to suit the story.

Norse Play 2

Peter Patterson

There sat Thrym firm on a mound, the king of the Giants and mas-ter of the frost.

Louder

Lea-shes of gold he laid for his dogs and stroked and smoothed the manes of his steeds.

Again, do be creative with your students and help them to make up more verses to fit the story. You can add more instruments, too, especially in the loud second part.

Poetic Edda

Peter Patterson

Hear-ing I ask from the ho-ly ra-ces, ___ from Heim-dall's sons, both high and low; ___ Thou wilt, Val-fa-ther, that well I re-late ___ old tales I re-mem-ber of men long a-go. ___ I re-mem-ber yet the gi-ants of yore, ___ who gave me bread in the days ___ gone by; ___ Nine worlds I knew, the nine in the tree ___ with migh-ty roots be-neath the mold. ___

This is the beginning of the Poetic or Elder Norse Edda, the mainstay of artistic experience in Class 4. The translation from the Icelandic is by Henry Adams Bellows, the only one I know that follows the rhythms and spirit of the original. You can add an accompaniment of a deep D, with higher As and Ds added, on any instruments you like. Just have one note or chord at the beginning of each bar, no more. Try inventing other chants of your own and make up musical interludes, which you can compose or the students can improvise. You might find this is much easier to do than you think - and the students will love doing it.

When you declaim by heart one or more whole books of the Edda with the students, which will have a lasting effect on the development of their personal energy and wellbeing, you will probably want to do it without music, but the experience of a page or so, sung to a chant like the above, will also help them to enter into the mood of Norse mythology.

In declaiming the Edda without music, remember there is one rhythmic pulse or stress in each half-line. The students can sometimes step (not stamp, please) forwards or backwards on that pulse. At other times they can practise stepping or doing eurythmic movements on the alliterative sounds. But above all, do practise a whole book by heart and not just little snippets, then the deeper energies of these magical texts can be released.

Sigurd and the Dragon

ed. Peter Patterson

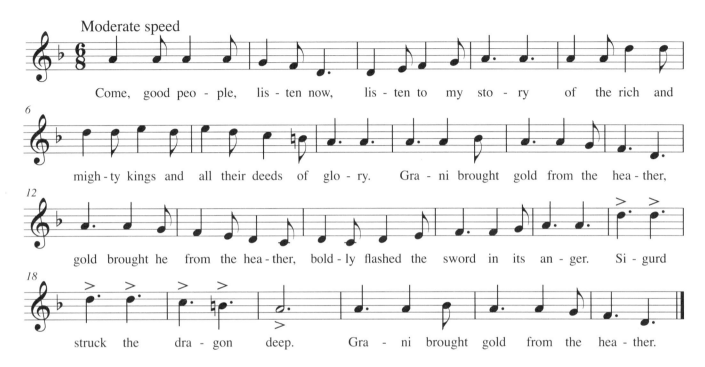

Moderate speed

Come, good peo - ple, lis - ten now, lis - ten to my sto - ry of the rich and

migh - ty kings and all their deeds of glo - ry. Gra - ni brought gold from the hea - ther,

gold brought he from the hea - ther, bold - ly flashed the sword in its an - ger. Si - gurd

struck the dra - gon deep. Gra - ni brought gold from the hea - ther.

2. On the gold the dragon lies,
   shrieking loud for vengeance;
   Sigurd rides on Grani's back,
   with his sword he threatens.
   Grani brought gold....
   (and so on in each verse)

3. Sigurd gave so great a thrust,
   'twas a mighty wonder;
   trembled every leaf and tree,
   the dragon roared like thunder....
   Grani brought gold....

4. Sigurd was so brave and bold,
   he that sword did brandish;
   cleft in twain the monster lay,
   the dead and glittering dragon....
   Grani brought gold....

This is a very old song from the Faroe Islands in the far north. It belongs particularly to Class 4 and their immersion into Norse mythology. It can be accompanied by instruments playing D and A, singly or as a drone.

Snow White

Peter Patterson

Rather slow and full-sounding

Snow White, Snow White, where do you roam?

In the sha - dy for - est now_____ there is your home;

there the lone - ly dwel - ling with dwarf or with gnome.

Snow White, Snow White, where do you roam?

This is a four-part round with sonorous harmonies, suitable for Class 4 upwards.

Celtic Blessing

old Scottish verse

Peter Patterson

A simple accompaniment can be improvised, based on Ds in the bass clef (keyboards or chimes) with As above them. The mood should be strong and powerful but very peaceful. Bells and gongs could also come into it, but again very simple. Accompany, do not distract from the chant.

Text from "The Sun Dances".

The Lord of Falkenstein

Translated and edited by Peter Patterson

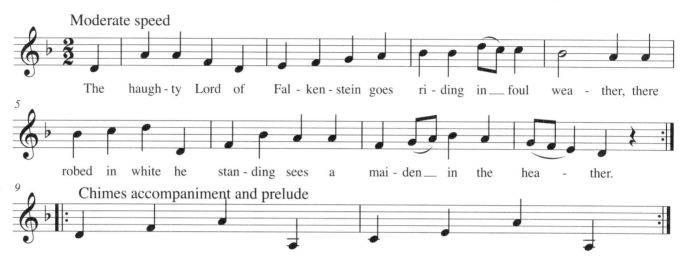

The two bars at the end are for chimes - metallophone or xylophone - and are used to introduce the song (two bars) and to accompany each verse. The accompaniment stops at the end of each verse then begins again at once, and so on, introducing each verse in the same way. The original is in German and is an old folk song. Here are the other verses:

2. [girls] "Are you the knight of Falkenstein,
   that lord of noble breeding?
   Then give to me my own true love,
   that we can make our wedding!"

3. [boys] "Within my castle stands a tower;
   that lover whom you cherish
   lies deep within each year and hour
   and there he'll most surely perish."

4. [girls] She stood and cried, "My dearest love's
   behind yon dark defences,
   and if my love I cannot have
   I soon must leave my senses."

5. [boys] "Then of your senses now take leave!
   Come, soldiers, end her wailing!
   Upon the walls your head shall stand,
   a spear your skull impaling!"

6. [girls] "As I'm a maid of valiant will
   I'm armed with sword and knife!
   These can I use with deadly skill,
   I'll fight with you for my true love's life!"

7. [boys] "With such a maiden I'll not strive,
   more honour lies in bounty.
   So I will give to you your love,
   flee with him from this county!"

Kalevala the chant lines

Peter Patterson

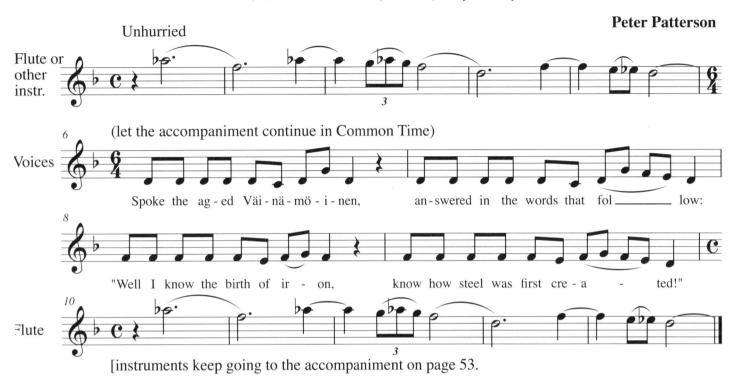

[instruments keep going to the accompaniment on page 53.

... now the next part of the text is chanted:

2. Air is the primeval mother,
   Water is the eldest brother,
   Iron is the youngest brother,
   In the middle stands the fire!
   [the flute interlude comes again]

3. Ukko, highest of creators,
   He the God above in heaven,
   From the air the water parted,
   From the water then the hard land,
   [use the first two bars of the chant now, and
   whenever the words go beyond the three bars]
   When as yet unborn was iron,
   yet unborn as yet ungrowing.
   [flute theme again]

If you want to chant more of the Iron Rune you will find it in Rune Nine of the Kalevala. Many parts of the epic could be learnt in this way. If you study the story of the epic with your students you should get Pekka Ervast's wonderful book, "The Key to the Kalevala", published by Blue Dolphin.

Kalevala accompaniment

Peter Patterson

This accompaniment is best performed on metallophones and xylophones. If you are not lucky enough to have such instruments around then you can use a piano (two players, four hands) or you could even try with strings, bowed, though the lowest part would sound great on a plucked double bass or an electric bass guitar (tune the lowest string down to D) if you perform the music with older students.

The first bar, repeated many times, is the basis of the Introduction. Play it four times, then bring in the solo flute, haunting and magical, as if from the distance.

When the chanting enters, change to the second bar of the instrumental parts, which is repeated as long as you want the chanting to continue. You must use a rhythmic translation of the Kalevala if you go beyond the Iron Rune lines that I have written here. The Penguin version keeps closely to the rhythms of the Finnish original.

The Kalevala epic is part of nordic mythology and we can use it in Class 4, but the poetry and music can also be used any time after that.

Kalevala interlude

Peter Patterson

Return at once, without any pause in the flow, to the original chant, the flute (the part that begins on A flat) playing quietly in the background. Don't worry about bar lines not fitting together with the 4/4 and 6/4, just let it fit together naturally.

The text of the next section of chant is:

2. There three maidens were created,
   Three fair daughters of creation,
   Mothers of the rusty iron,
   Givers of the blue-mouthed steel.

3. Swinging then, the maids a-moving,
   On the clouds' edge they were striding,
   Down to earth their milk was flowing,
   In the earth, in swampy marshes,
   Milk into the peaceful waters.

[Just repeat a phrase of the music to accommodate the extra line]

Now the day has come

Peter Patterson

Brightly

1. Now the day has come greet we ev-'ry one, let us all be mer-ry whe-ther rain or sun!

2. Work shall be joy, play shall be fun, yes, whe-ther we are sit-ting or a-round we run.

3. Gree-tings to___ ev-'ry one, whe-ther in rain___ or___ sun.

2. Stars shone in our sleep from the heavens deep,
   shining angels walked around us safe to keep.
   Tasks shall we do, though paths be steep,
   yes, whether we go slowly or with joy we leap.
   Greetings to everyone, whether in rain or sun.

This is a three-part round but can also be sung as a song in plain unison.

The Golden Time

Trad. German + Peter Patterson

2. When the apple tree lets its blossom fall,
   when the swallow's flying and the cuckoos call,
   all the birds are nesting, never pause for resting,
   then begins the lovely golden time.

This amazingly joyful little canon is from Germany, labelled "traditional", though some happy person must have composed it, for canons don't just evolve naturally. As you can see, the second voice comes in after just two eighth notes (quavers). I have translated the words into English and added a bass part, which gives the harmonies more grunt. Be aware that the second verse comes without any pause at all, as do any repeats. As it is a canon (as distinct from a round) the second voice must finish by itself, not together with the first voice.

The Golden Time, bass part

Peter Patterson

This added bass line is intended to be sung, but it can also be played on any bass instrument. The most important thing to know about it is that it only enters with the second voice and not with the first!

Coffee Song

German trad., trans. Patterson

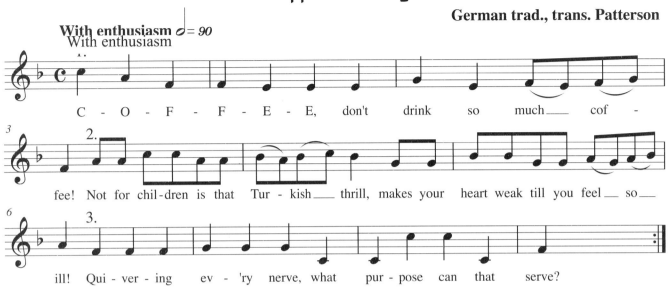

With enthusiasm ♩= 90

C - O - F - F - E - E, don't drink so much___ cof -

fee! Not for chil-dren is that Tur - kish___ thrill, makes your heart weak till you feel __ so__

ill! Qui - ver - ing ev - 'ry nerve, what pur - pose can that serve?

This traditional German round is a very great favourite and will always be sung with verve even when the children are tired; so it is useful to have an English version.

Flying Song

Peter Patterson

Leisurely but not slow

1. Flip - pet - y swish - et - y off we shall go fly - ing on wings with the eag - le and crow.

2. Flip - pet - y swish - et - y watch us all fly ov - er the roof tops and in - to the sky.

3. We can all do it if we try!

2. Flippety swishety watch us with ease
   swoop like young swallows high over the trees!
   Flippety swishety into the blue,
   such an adventure for me and for you!
   We can all do it,
   that is true!

This flying song was written to be sung whenever a boost of confidence might be helpful - such as at the beginning of a mathematics lesson! And what better way to boost confidence than singing!

It is a three-part round but can equally well be sung in unison as a plain song.

Acrobat

Peter Patterson

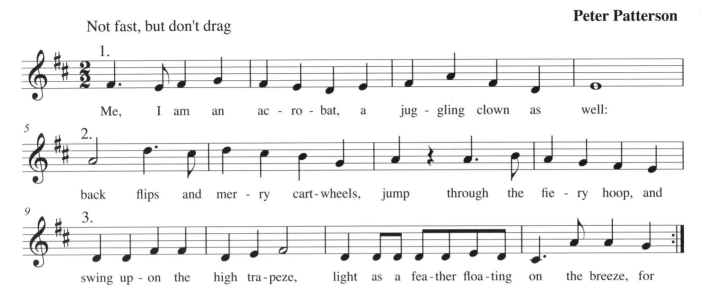

Not fast, but don't drag

Me, I am an ac - ro - bat, a jug - gling clown as well:

back flips and mer - ry cart-wheels, jump through the fie - ry hoop, and

swing up - on the high tra - peze, light as a fea - ther floa - ting on the breeze, for

This is a three-part round and it can go round several times, but when it stops it could be on the notes at the beginning of each entry, on "me", "back" and "swing" to form the chord of D major.

Joyous is the Day

Peter Patterson

Joyously but without hurrying

Joy - ous is the day, let us be a ray shi - ning on the way of ev' - ry - one we meet this ____ day!

This is a three-part round to begin the day. You might find one verse is enough, but here are some more anyway:

2. Golden shines the sun both on work and fun,
   shining while we're working
   or around the world we run.

3. Silver gleams the moon getting rid of gloom,
   bringing light to darkness
   for she knows the dawn comes soon.

4. Gleaming shines each star, healing wound or scar
   from when joy had left us
   and was absent long and far.

5. On the river flows, on the pathway goes
   through the highest mountains
   as my heart in goodness grows.

Pretty Colours

Peter Patterson

Joyfully

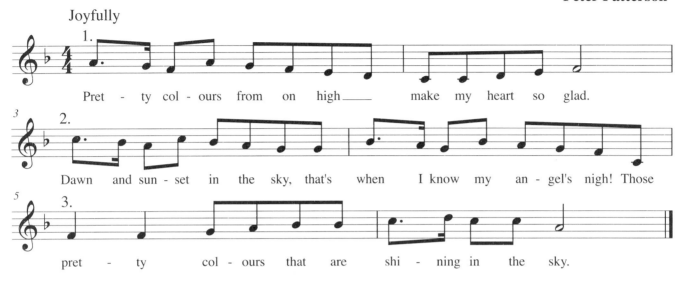

Pret - ty col - ours from on high___ make my heart so glad.

Dawn and sun - set in the sky, that's when I know my an - gel's nigh! Those

pret - ty col - ours that are shi - ning in the sky.

This 3-part round is easy to sing. I wrote it while watching a wonderful sunset in New Zealand

62

Old Tom's Songbadil

Peter Patterson

This tune has been loved by generations of Waldorf children, especially around the age of 10 to 11 but also much later. You could sing the many verses to this tune that Tom Bombadil chants. There are very many such verses so you have a wide choice! I have written guitar or harp chords in, too.

Song of the Nature Spirits

Peter Patterson

Please note: there are no sharps or flats in this tune.

2. Earth, water, fire, and air
   weave the body that you wear!
   The Mother and Maiden, old and fair,
   bid you answer if you dare:
   all the world must learn to share.
   Earth, water, fire, and air
   weave the body.

Song of the Nature Spirits 2

Peter Patterson

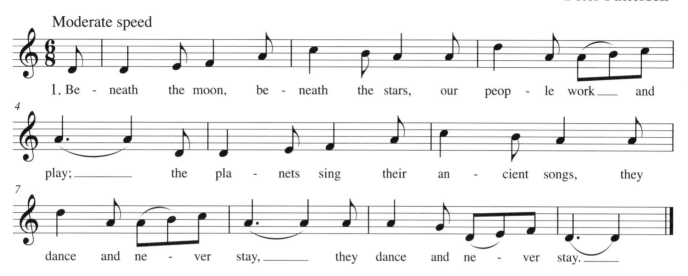

1. Be - neath the moon, be - neath the stars, our peop - le work ___ and play; ___ the pla - nets sing their an - cient songs, they dance and ne - ver stay, ___ they dance and ne - ver stay.

2. The light that shines beneath the stars
   is of a gentler ray;
   the voices of the trees and stones
   are lost by light of day,
   are lost by light of day.

3. We help your children when we can,
   for children too are we;
   your hearts must grow the sun to know
   that shines beyond the sea,
   beyond the enchanted sea.

4. The sea, the sea, the enchanted sea!
   Beyond your world are lands
   where friend and enemy alike
   are joined with golden bands,
   are joined with golden bands!

65

Song of the Nature Spirits 3

Peter Patterson

This tune, with its unusual scale of C natural and G sharp, has been very popular in Classes 4 and 5, and I have also found it awakens a friendly awareness and response when played on a pipe or sung to trees in a forest. Notice that in bars 3, 7, and 10 the G# of the tune clashes intentionally with the C natural in the accompaniment. It can be sung to the song that Legolas sings when the Fellowship escapes from Moria. There, it refers to the spirit of a waterfall.

Song of the Nature Spirits 4

Not too fast

Peter Patterson

This dwarfs' song is probably my most popular song of all. It could be sung to the words that the dwarfs sing when they first visit the Shire and Hobbiton, but for copyright reasons they cannot be printed here. There are many verses.

The Interlude is best played on a pipe or recorder. I have added guitar chords but they could also be played on a Celtic harp.

Birds

Peter Patterson

Please be very careful to note that this is not an ordinary major scale. The C (in "never let you be", for example) is always a C#, never C natural.

The flute (or recorder) parts begin first, as their own two-part round, and continue throughout. Then the glockenspiel is added and also continues, then the xylophone (or plucked cello). Last of all the singers come in with the three part round, accompanied by everyone else.

Let the children make up other verses for themselves - but here are two more suggestions:

2. Wagtail, wagtail, wagtail, wagtail,
   bob along the brook,
   fly upon that old tree stump,
   to get a better look!
   Bob, wagtail, bob, wagtail,
   by the brook.

3. Starling, starling, starling, starling,
   glistening in the sun,
   imitate your neighbour's calling,
   there's no better fun.
   Call, starling, call, starling,
   in the sun.

Hymn to the Dawn

ed. Peter Patterson

Lively, but unhurried

North India

[Introduction and interlude between the verses]

She has shone bright - ly full of beau - ty __ stir - ring ev - 'ry - liv - ing
Lea - ding her cour - ser white and fair to __ look on, bear - ing the

crea - ture __ of the world; Ra - diant with gol - den col - ours,
gods' own __ true bright eye; Bring - ing her trea - sures from be -

moth - er __ of the cat - tle wak - ing in the __ mor - ning dew;
yond the __ world __ in her love - ly arms __ there on high.

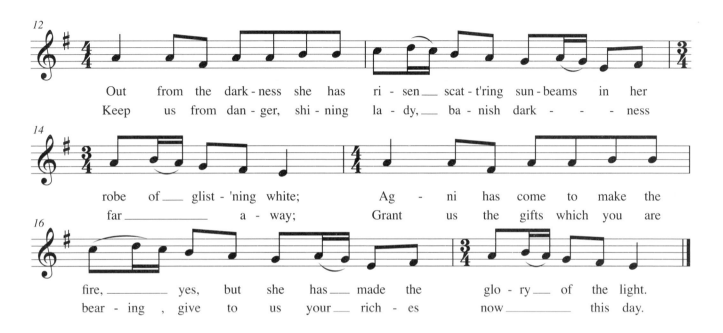

Out from the dark-ness she has ri - sen— scat - t'ring sun-beams in her
Keep us from dan - ger, shi - ning la - dy,— ba - nish dark - - - ness

robe of — glist - 'ning white; Ag — ni has come to make the
far _____ a - way; Grant us the gifts which you are

fire, _____ yes, but she has — made the glo - ry — of the light.
bear - ing , give to us your — rich - es now _____ this day.

Go straight into the interlude without pause and then into the second verse.

Play the interlude again... You need some fast and very precise drumming to accompany this piece, which I have transformed from a North Indian folksong (from Uttar Pradesh). A double-ended drum would be ideal but I have heard a child in India do brilliant drumming on a metal tea-tray! Use what you can find, raid the kitchen!

Vedic chant - to Vishnu

It is characteristic of Class 5 (age 10) to do exciting blocks of various mythologies.
Here is a chant to the creator-god Vishnu, sung unaccompanied.

arr. Peter Patterson

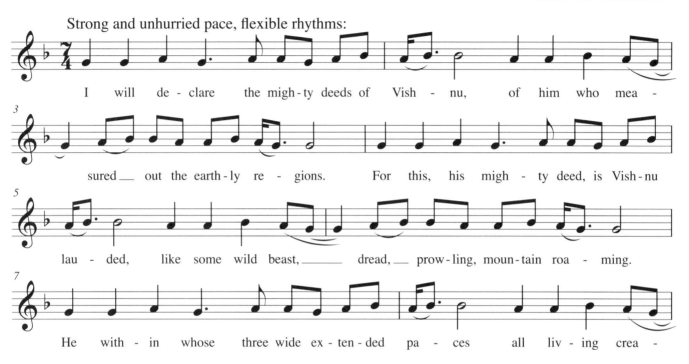

Strong and unhurried pace, flexible rhythms:

I will de - clare the migh - ty deeds of Vish - nu, of him who mea -

sured out the earth - ly re - gions. For this, his migh - ty deed, is Vish - nu

lau - ded, like some wild beast, dread, prow - ling, moun - tain roa - ming.

He with - in whose three wide ex - ten - ded pa - ces all liv - ing crea -

tures __ have their ha - bi - ta - tion. Let the hymn lift it - self as strength to

Vish - nu, the bull, far stri - ding, __ dwel - ling on the moun - tains.

Who ve - ri - ly a - lone up - holds the three - fold: the earth, the hea -

vens, __ and all liv - ing crea - tures. May I at - tain to that, his well - loved

man - sion, where folk de - vo - ted __ to the gods are hap - py.

Gayatri Mantra

Indian traditional

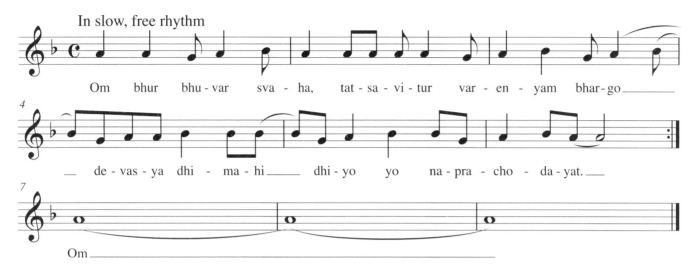

In slow, free rhythm

Om bhur bhu - var sva - ha, tat - sa - vi - tur var - en - yam bhar-go___

___ de - vas - ya dhi - ma - hi___ dhi - yo yo na - pra - cho - da - yat. ___

Om ___

For each of the mythologies, history, and geography studies we do at school it makes a big difference if we can use suitable music to deepen the students' immersion and pleasure. For the Indian mythology of Class 5 this mantra of light, the Gayatri mantra, is most helpful. Each area of India appears to have its own melody, but the one on this page was sung to me by an educated Hindu colleague in Tridha, the Mumbai Waldorf School, who assured me it was a version that is widespread.

As a mantra, to enter properly into the calm state of mind intended, it should be sung at least 108 times without pause! But you will be anxious to get on with the Main Lesson and DO something, no doubt - a very "western" feeling! You should set a goal, though, in chanting a mantra, even if it's only 18 times instead of 108!

A word about pronunciation. In the consonants which we transliterate as bh and dh, we need to hear the h distinctly, so for example bhur sounds almost like bahoor, and dhi is almost dahee. Ch is just like English ch in church or cheerful. Ur is always oor, never 'er'. The o in Om is a big round o, like in 'home'. Om is said to be the sound God made when creating the universe. At the end of the recitation the Om should be sounded as long as possible - on one breath!

Egyptian Dance

Peter Patterson

Continued over....

Du - wan   du - wan   du - wan   du - wan e - zi!_____   A -

kwar 'n - ti di te - na,   a - kwar 'n ti di te - na,   a - kwar 'n ti di te - na,   a - kwar!_____

A - kwar 'n - ti di te - na,   a - kwar 'n ti di te - na,   a - kwar 'n ti di te - na,   a -

Continue repeating the song as long as the dancing continues.... You can add other instruments too, like a systrum (rattle of metal discs) and for the bass instrument they used large harps. Invent a dance and use the music for movement.

This dance is especially for the Ancient Egyptian block in Class 5 but can be used at any time in the years that follow. By practising music of other cultures that has scales and rhythms different from our western stereotypes the children learn to listen to all types of music more keenly. If you are lucky enough to have a bass instrument, add a deep G to every first beat and the D below to the second beat of each bar. The children will be 'unstoppable'!

The words mean: Go forth to the land (countryside) to stretch out (to relax).
Precious is that which you give (as a farewell gift). ('Ezi' means 'go forth'. 'Tena' means 'you'.)

Hymn to U-si-re

Peter Patterson

With vigorous energy

Shout a - loud, you peo - ple who with - in the tem - ple stand: Glo - ry
to om - ni - po - tent U - si - - re! Bla - zen forth his tri - umph till his
splen - dour fills the land; hon - our to the liv - ing God, U - si - - re!

2. Secret is his nature and his ways beyond our ken,
   ancient, yet a babe is great_ Usire!
   As the Moon he wa_tches the months for men,
   times and seasons wait upon_ Usire!

3. When the Sun god passes to the realms of death and night
   monarch of that kingdom is_ Usire!
   When he comes in glory in the glowing morning light,
   throned on high beside him is Usire!

4. When the river rises, bringing happiness and mirth,
   as the joyous Nile we hail Usire!
   Giver of the harvest and creator of the Earth,
   all we have and are is from_ Usire!

5. Women, hymn his triumph! Let your voices, men, ring out,
   cry aloud all creatures of_ Usire!
   Thunder forth his praises in one vast triumphant shout,
   "Glory to the Risen Lord_, Usire!

This is a song for the Egyptian mythology of Class 5, though it can be performed later, too. The first and third lines of each verse are sung by the "priests" or "priestesses", just two or three children who face the others. The rest of the class or group sing the second and fourth lines very loudly and enthusiastically.

Add drums to increase the vigour: a deep drum, just one thump at the beginning and middle of each bar. Smaller drums place eighth notes (quavers), syncopated if possible, to raise the excitement. A single deep base note (double bass or keyboard) sounds on E at the beginning of each bar only. Rattles (systrums) can also add to the energy.

Gilgamesh

Peter Patterson

The percussion (deep drum and/or hand drum) plays throughout on every half-note (minim) beat, creating a cross-rhythm in the first seven bars but then coinciding with the singers in the eight bars following. If you use the song as a processional, the students step on the same beats that they hear from the drum(s), so they are singing and walking in cross-rhythm. Yes, quite tricky but once they can do it they will find it easy - I promise you!

2. Ah, Enkidu, now from great kingdoms of light
   Return to your friend, will you pity his plight?
   May Anu keep us, Shamash bright
   Protect us with heavenly light.

3. The King must now wander, forever a guest;
   The whole world awaits him in north, south, east, and west.
   May Anu keep us, Shamash bright
   Protect us with heavenly light.

4. We also want certainty, knowledge we pursue;
   This, too, is our quest, seeking wisdom that is true.
   May Anu keep us, Shamash bright
   Protect us with heavenly light.

Searching Satyrs 1

Peter Patterson

Vigorous ♩= 100

When the sound of the lyre gets ___ hold of my heels, all my bo - dy takes fire till it stag - gers and reels; ___ a - way and a - way to the mad - ding sweet sound till our bo - dies grow wear - ried and sink to the ground. ___

2. Now my feet cannot cease nor my legs be at rest,
for the wild strains increase, and increases my zest.
I long not for love, and I crave not for wine -
let me live, let me die, with this music divine!

This is the first of three songs for the little religious comedy, the "Ichneutai", or Searching Satyrs, by Sophokles (adapted from Rieu's translation in Penguin Books). You can see that the scale I have used (from below it is C D E F# G A B-flat C) is neither the western major nor the minor scale most of us are used to. From at least Class 5 on I get the students used to scales other than the ones they hear on the radio in order to diversify and expand their hearing. They quickly adapt and begin humming the tunes as naturally as the rather overworked western scales.

This play is great fun in Classes 5 or 6.

Searching Satyrs 3

Peter Patterson

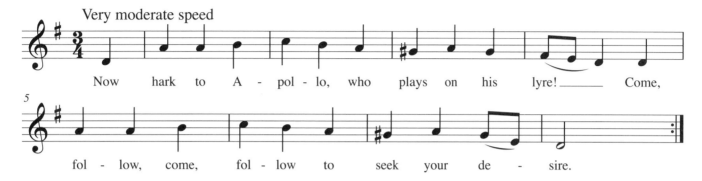

2. With music delighting the children of day
   Apollo is lighting the world on its way.

3. Apollo, Apollo is speeding and leading
   the dance of my days out by valley and hill.

4. Sweet, sweet the desire in my heart that is breeding;
   I gasp with delight as the lyre sounds shrill.

5. I follow Apollo, his leading, go speeding
   away and away he is leading me still.

This dance is a processional that leads the actors off the stage and out of sight.

Again, note the scale: D E F# G# A B C D. It is the scale of the great First Delphic Hymn, so it is suitable for the solemn ending of what has been a funny and entertaining play. Originally it was written for a festival in Delphi itself, to be performed in the amphitheatre, so although it is a comedy it has an underlying serious intention: to symbolise the union of the Apollonian and Dyonysian streams in the Delphic temple mysteries.

Searching Satyrs 2 is over the page....

Searching Satyrs 2

Peter Patterson

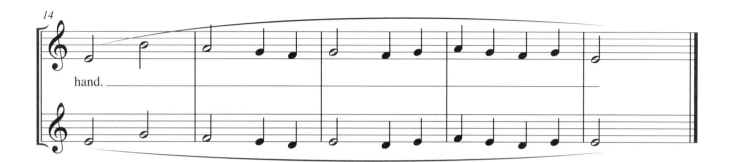

Singing in parallel thirds, or even seconds, is an ancient practice in the northern Mediterranean cultures and can still be found in some rural districts today, for instance in Croatia. Again, be aware of the scale: F is always NATURAL.

The students can learn to dance in a circle in the old way. An accompaniment of E and the B above, once a bar, can be played on lyre, harp, or chimes, and if all that fails, then cello (pizz.) is better than nothing.

Even if you cannot fit this play into your year plan, you can still do the songs and dances in connection with the Greek myths (Class 5 or beginning of 6).

Roman Music 1

Peter Patterson

The first seven bars are sung by everyone, without accompaniment. After a silence the instruments begin with two bars introduction, then the shorter song (between the repeat marks) is added, first in unison, then after a pause (in which the instruments keep going), as a four-part round. The Romans did not sing rounds and this music is not meant to be in imitation of what they may have sung but is intended to give some musical colour to history lessons. The words are from an angry poem by the Roman poet Catullus.

When the singers finish, the players give one last crash on their instruments, centering on D, but with some As too.

Roman Song

accompaniment

Peter Patterson

Lines 1 and 2 should be played on wind instruments, recorders, flutes, or oboes.
Line 3 can be played on chimes, metal or wooden; and the bass line on anything convenient!

Ancient Greek Dance

Peter Patterson

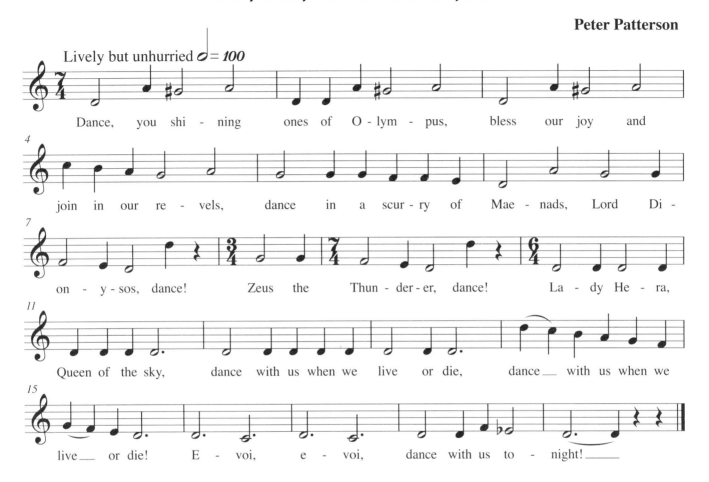

The percussion players, tambourine and cymbals, perhaps also a hand drum, must be very supportive of the changes of duple and triple beats. They must learn to drive the dance rhythms but not hurry them.

This song can be used as a real ring dance, being played on instruments together with the singing, then again with it, alternating.

"Evoi!" was the ecstatic shout of the cult of Dionysos.

Birds are Winging

Peter Patterson

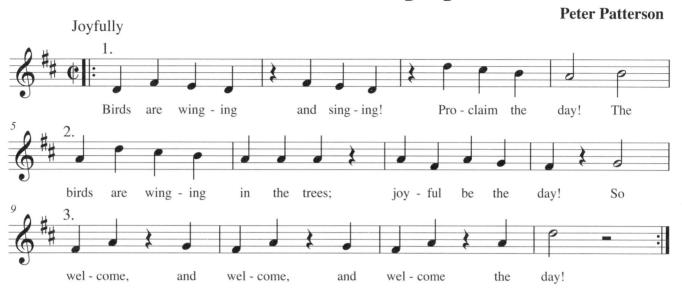

This is an easy three-part round to sing first thing in the morning to get people breathing. It can be sung as a unison song or in parts; from Class Three onwards. Choose your own chord to finish on.

Sadness and Mirth

Peter Patterson

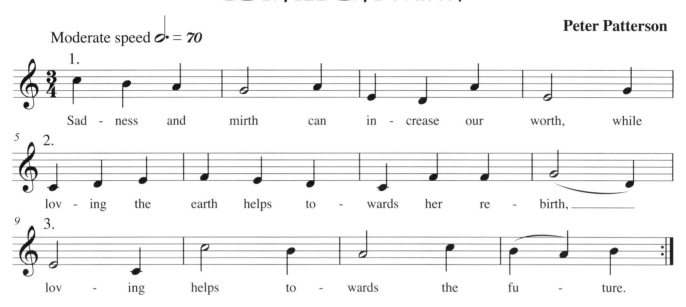

Moderate speed ♩. = 70

Sad - ness and mirth can in - crease our worth, while

lov - ing the earth helps to - wards her re - birth, _____

lov - ing helps to - wards the fu - ture.

This is a simple three-part round, suitable for beginning a meal, a walk together, a history lesson, whatever. On which notes will you stop? I like the conductor to choose, but in this case it need be no secret that the first note of each entry (under the numbers) is a good choice for a final chord.

All is Silent

Mozart, trans. P. Patterson

Restful and melodious ♩ = *100*

1. All is si – lent – through all the val – ley.

2. Nigh – tin – gales sing – ing such sweet me – lo – dies,
tears come un – bid – den, long – ing and joy.

3. Nigh – tin – gales sing – ing such sweet me – lo – dies,
tears come un – bid – den, long – ing and joy.

This very beautiful three part round (four bars between each entry) that can be best sung from
Class 6 onwards.

The Lord, We Say

Karl Marx, ed./trans. P.P.

The Lord, we say, is ri - sen; the Lord, we say, is tru - ly a - ri - sen,

Hal - le - lu - ia, hal - le - lu - ia! The Lord, we say, is

This attractive canon was written by Karl Marx - not the author of Das Kapital but a German musician who wrote many pieces for amateur singers. The upper accompaniment (which I have changed somewhat as a result of using the piece with many groups) can be played on recorders or on whatever is at hand. When you want to finish, stop on the last note of the Halleluias, but being a canon (not a round) each of the two voices must complete their tune.

Merry Let Us Be

Round.

Peter Patterson

Merrily, but not too fast

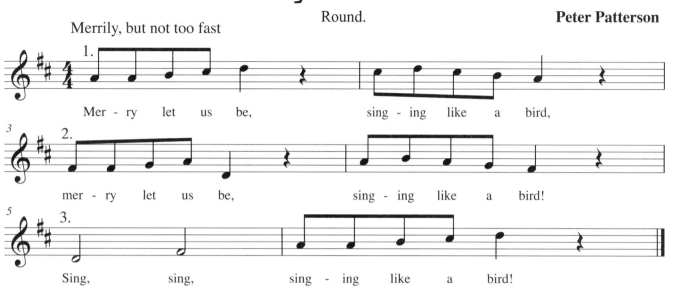

Mer - ry let us be, sing - ing like a bird,

mer - ry let us be, sing - ing like a bird!

Sing, sing, sing - ing like a bird!

Swallows

Peter Patterson

Well, the birds deserve a three-part round, too. And why are the swallows so high in the sky? Only in good weather, when the insects fly high and the swallows follow them. When they fly close to the ground it's a sign of bad weather.

The Elven Halleluia

Peter Patterson

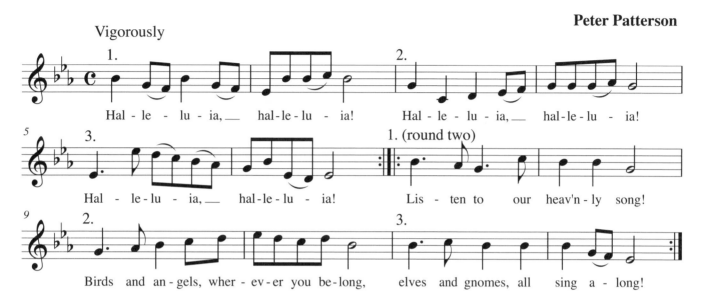

These are two separate rounds which can be sung together or separately. If you want to sing them together, begin by getting the Halleluia going strongly, then bring "Listen to..." in while the Halleluia becomes much quieter. The "Listen to..." can also be sung as a solo, not as a round at all. Either way, let the "Listen to..." end and bring the volume of the Halleluia back up to a fortissimo!

Remember that rounds, as distinct from canons, should always finish on a chord, all together, not by letting each voice finish its part.

Michael, the Victorious

Peter Patterson

Moderate but with vigour ♩ = 80

1. Thou Mi - cha - el, the Vic - tor - i - ous, I make my cir - cuit un - der thy shield. Thou Mi - cha - el of the white steed, and of the bright bril - liant blade,

Faster

con - quer - or of the dra - gon, be thou at my back.

2. Thou ranger of the heavens,
   thou warrior of the King of All,
   O Michael, the victorious,
   my pride and my guide!
   Michael, the victorious, the glory of mine eye!

3. Though I should travel the ocean
   and all the hard lands of the world,
   no harm can ever befall me
   beneath the shelter of thy shield.
   Michael, the victorious, the jewel of my heart!

Michael Song 2

With vigour ♩= 70

Peter Patterson

Words by Cecil Harwood

2. Frost on the ground as misty dawning shines bright,
   cracking the clod, lining the twigs with white.
   Sleepers, awake! Hark to the word of the frost.... (Continue as in the first verse)

3. Myriad stars shine in the frosty, clear skies,
   outshining all, the meteor earthward flies.
   Sleepers, awake! Hark to the word of the stars....

4. With hearts aglow we mark the changing fresh world,
   when from the stars Michael's spear is hurled.
   Sleepers awake! Hark to the word of the world....

Michael Song 3

Peter Patterson

With strength ♩ = *80*

The time has come! The time has come! Thus sounds it

in our hearts. It is the time of Mi - cha - el, who

o - ver - comes and guards, who o - ver - comes and guards.

2. Our task is now to transform light
   into the power of love.
   The temple, which was long below,
   can now be found above, can now be found above.

3. Great angels will bestow their gifts
   on every one who strives.
   A bridge across the river be
   the aim of all our lives, the aim of all our lives.

4. Our future now is ours to shape,
   our own true self to find,
   for Michael's lamp is shining bright
   to guide all human kind, to guide all human kind.

Words adapted by Benedict Wood from Goethe's Fairy Tale of "The Green Snake and the Beautiful Lily".

Table Blessing Alleluia

Peter Patterson

Moderate speed ♩ = 85

Earth, who gives to us this food, sun, who made it ripe and — good: Dear

earth, dear sun, by you — we — live, our lov - ing thanks to you we give!

Al - le - lu - ia! Al - le - lu - - ia!

Al - le - lu - ia, _____ al - le - lu - ia, a - men!

The Song of the Road

Peter Patterson

Moderate, but with a lively tread

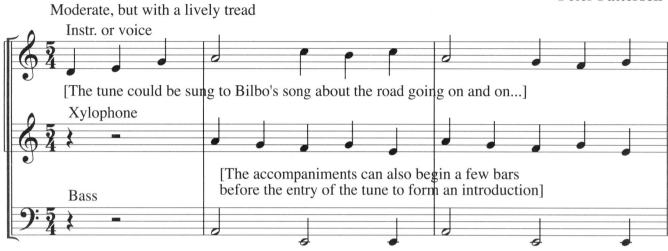

[The tune could be sung to Bilbo's song about the road going on and on...]

[The accompaniments can also begin a few bars
before the entry of the tune to form an introduction]

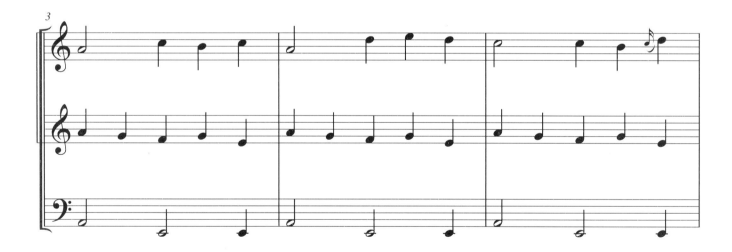

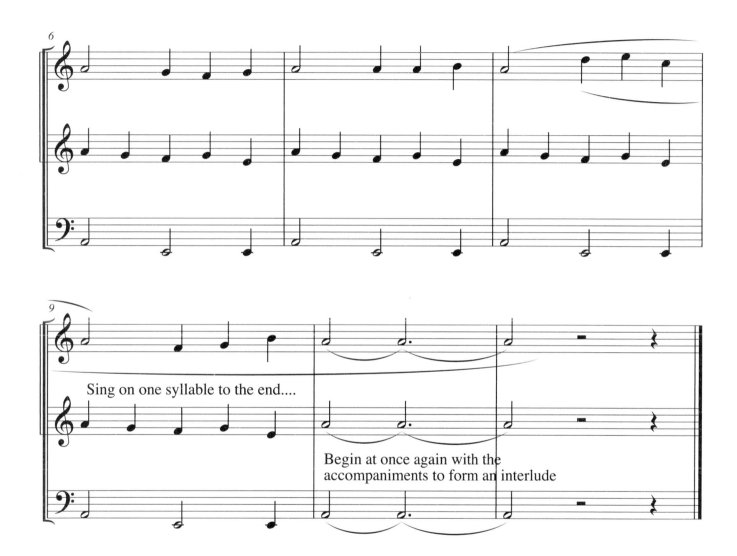

Sing on one syllable to the end....

Begin at once again with the
accompaniments to form an interlude

Rhythm Round

Peter Patterson

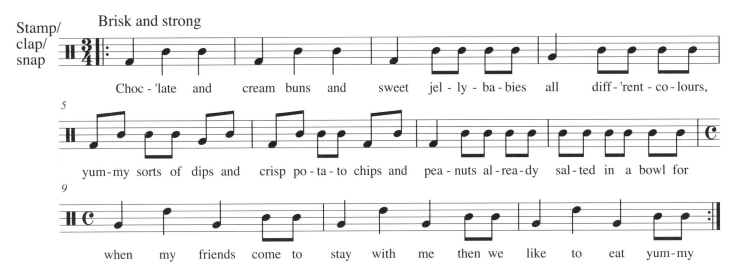

Rhythm rounds are great fun and teach us to be aware of time values and of one another.
Use stamping, clapping, finger snap (lowest note, middle note, top note in the score), or percussion
(like bongos), or just speak in exact time - or all three at once! Even tapping on pots and pans makes
a welcome change from the sound of accustomed instruments.

This is just an example of the infinite possibilities of rhythm work - to encourage you and the
students to make up such rounds of your own. It can be done while working at learning to read and
count time values, which many find harder to do than read the pitch values of notes.

Bulgarian dance rhythms

Peter Patterson

Continued over....

mor - row   the   cob - ler's   men   bright   and   ear - ly!

Xyl.

Met.

Bass

2. Drum and cymbal ringing, merriment a-bringing,
   out our troubles flinging!
   Here come some gypsy folk ready for prank and joke,
   gaily singing!

3. Can you see our mayor there, leading pair by pair there?
   What a fellow rare there!
   How he can leap and prance, no one else stands a chance,
   that's not quite fair!

Exaltate

Double round

Lassus, ed. Patterson

Moderate speed but not slow

I have composed this double round from elements gleaned from a more difficult composition by the Late Renaissance composer known as Orlandus Lassus, though his actual German name has a different sound. Lassus was a master of resonant accoustic effects created by clever part-writing. This version can be tackled by a high school class or choir, best using instruments to double and support the singers' voices, the usual practice in the Renaissance. If the second round can be sung an octave lower by male voices, so much the better.

You can let the first round get established before bringing in the second, two-part, round, or you can start them off at the same time. Work out your own place to stop, but remember as this is a round, as distinct from a canon, all parts stop together on one chord.

Funky Greeting

Peter Patterson

Here come we, that's you and — me, so glad that you're a - round!

Here come we, that's you and me, so glad that — you're a - round! ——— I real-ly

am be - cause it's you and me!

This three-part round goes well with Class 7 upwards, especially if you have a deep bass instrument to play its lowest E and D (in time with the last section) to sound strongly throughout - but bring the bass in only when the second entry comes (the "2.").

Gelmindel

Peter Patterson

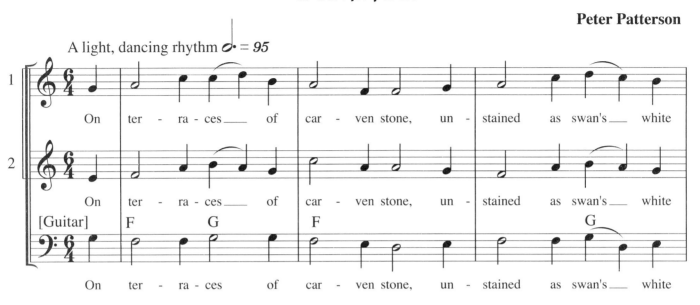

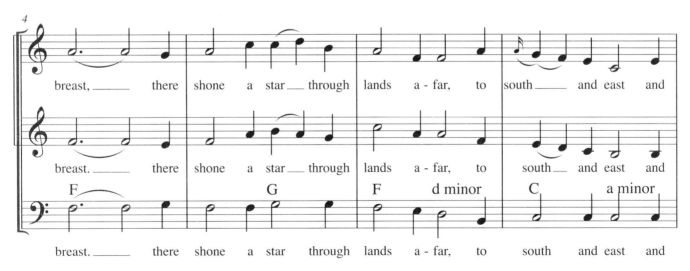

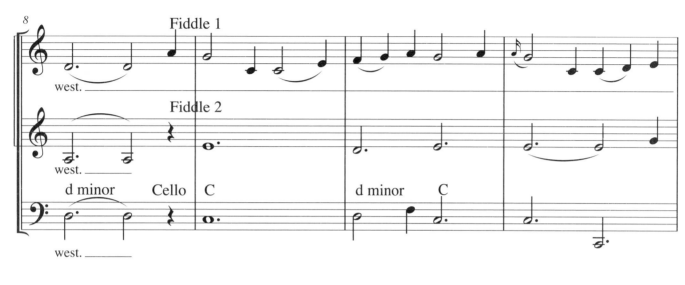

continued over....

107

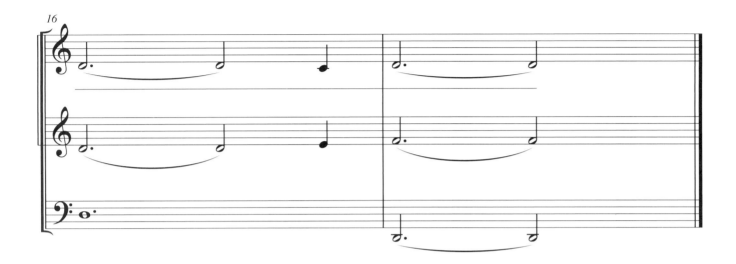

2. The streams that ran from fountains clear, the waterfalls that fell,
   made rainbow veils of sparkling light in ancient Gelmindel.

3. There dragons walked about her streets and danced by fountains fair
   to music played on silver pipes by elves with shining hair.

4. Now broken are the marble walls, and we have said farewell
   to fountains of the dancing light that shone in Gelmindel.

Gloria Deo

Peter Patterson

This is an assertive, three part round, four bars between each entry.
End together, each part on its fourth bar as its final note.
It could be sung from Class 6 upwards.

Music from West Africa

Class 7 upwards

arr. Peter Patterson

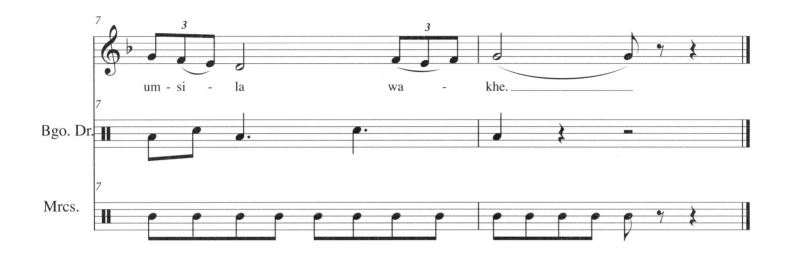

Begin the accompaniment before the song enters, letting the rhythm get well into a steady stride first. Continue with the instruments throughout, including between verses if you want to make a break between bars 4 and 5, and if you want to repeat from the beginning to make a longer piece of it. The persistent rhythm of the instruments should have a magical, almost hypnotic effect. The same advice applies to "Evua", the second African chant.

West Africa 2: Evua, the Sun God

arr. Peter Patterson

Begin the song again after all percussion players have had a good session. Remember: clear, EXACT playing!

Continue...

Continue...

Continue...

Xylophones (wooden) are typical of parts of West Africa. Let Xylophone 1 begin alone, then add Xyl. 2, then the other parts. After a while the singers begin. The Tenor Drum part is really easy, actually it is just 'Long- - short short'.

113

Joyous Alleluia

13th Century, arr. P. Patterson

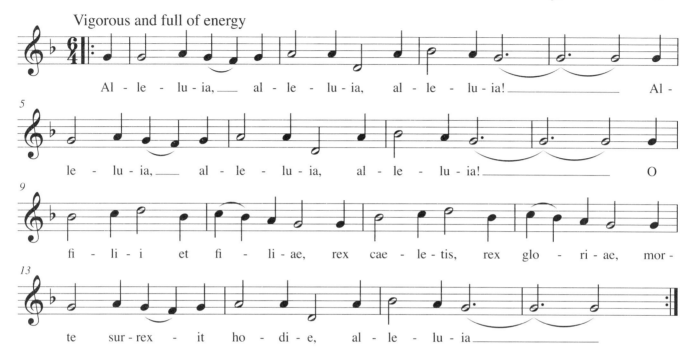

Al - le - lu - ia, ___ al - le - lu - ia, al - le - lu - ia! ___ Al -

le - lu - ia, ___ al - le - lu - ia, al - le - lu - ia! ___ O

fi - li - i et fi - li - ae, rex cae - le - tis, rex glo - ri - ae, mor -

te sur - rex - it ho - di - e, al - le - lu - ia ___

2. Discipulis adstantibus, in medio stetit Christus dicens: "Pax vobis omnibus!" Alleluia!

3. Ut intellexit Didymus quia surrexat Jesus remansit fere dubius, Alleluia!

4. Vide, Thomas, vide latus, vide pedes, vide manus, noli esse incredulus, Alleluia!

5. In hoc festo sanctissimo sit laus et jubilatio! Benedicamus domino, Alleluia!

[Prose translation, not for singing:
1. O sons and daughters, the king of heaven, king of glory, has risen from the dead today, Alleluia!
2. The disciples were standing around, in the middle was the Christ, saying: "Peace to all of you!" Alleluia!
3. So that the twin could understand that Jesus had risen, his doubts were removed, Alleluia!
4. Look, Thomas, look at the wounds, look at the feet, look at the hands, do not be incredulous, Alleluia!
5. In this most sacred festival may there be praise and jubilation; bless the Lord, Alleluia!]

Joyous Alleluia accompaniments

Peter Patterson

Vigorous, following the singers

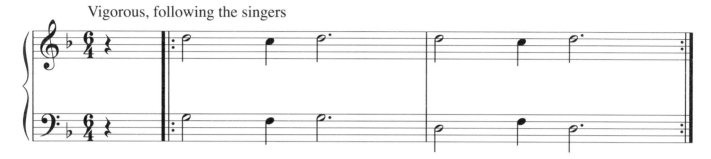

The ostinato accompaniment above supports the repeated Alleluia bars before each verse of the song but then falls silent as the verses tell the story. Those Alleluia bars can be quite loud and rollicking. The two parts can be played on any instruments, recorders or whatever, but trumpets and trombones would sound just wonderful. Tambourines, rattles, and drums can punctuate twice in a bar too, on every dotted half-note (minim), and this can continue very softly during the verses, coming in with a crash when we return to the Alleluia refrain.

Notice that parts moving in parallel fifths (in the accompaniment) are typical in medieval music in Europe. They fell out of favour later, in the fourteenth century.

Mystic Alleluia

Peter Patterson

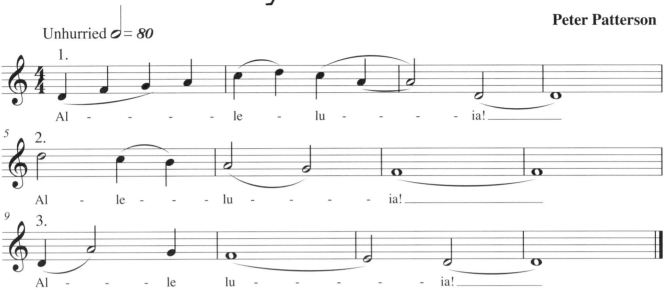

This is a demanding round for older students who have had some experience in getting sustained harmonies really in tune. The conductor needs to encourage the singers not to breathe all at the same time but individually and randomly in order to maintain the calm, contemplative effect.

Splendid Alleluia

Peter Patterson

Calmly but not without strength and vigour

The __ Lord __ is __ tru - ly __ ri - sen! Al - le - lu - ia, al - le - lu - ia,

al - le - lu - ia, __ al - le - lu - ia, __ al - le - lu - ia! A - men. The __

[Instruments only. Begin on the repeat of the song, not from the beginning]

Finish on the chord with the F sharp in it.

The harmonies of this Easter round can sound especially splendid if the 4-bar instrumental round is added to it. Trumpets would be ideal!

Antigone chorus 1

Entry processional, actors and musicians

Peter Patterson
(music and text translation)

In a firm and strong march time

1. Hail the sun the ___ brigh - test of all that ev - er ___ dawned on the ci - ty of

Se - ven Gates! ___ Hail the gol - den ___ dawn ov - er Dir - ke's riv - er, ri - sing to speed the

white in - va - ders home - ward in full re - treat! 2. Po - li - ni - kes had or - dered his

ar - my a - gainst ___ us, in an - gry dis - pute his proud shou - ting was heard; ___ like a

ra - ven - ing vul - ture he swooped all a - round ___ us with white wings a - flash - ing, with

fly - ing plumes, ___ his great ar - my ad - vanced rank on rank.

3. By the seven gates of Thebes in a circle of blood
   His sharp swords stood all round us, his jaws opened wide,
   But before he could wound us or burn us with fire
   He fled with the roar of the dragon behind him
   And thunder of war in his ears.

4. The Father of heaven hates the proud tongue's boasting,
   Was watching the torrent, the flashing stream
   Of their golden harness, the clash of their weapons,
   He heard them cry "Victory!" over our ramparts
   And smote them with fire to the ground.

(They all shout) The god fights for us! (A silence.... then faster, speaking rhythmically) Great is the victory, great the joy, in the city of Thebes, the city of chariots. Now is the time to fill the temples with glad thanksgiving of warfare ended. Shake the ground with the night-long dances, Bacchus afoot and delight abounding. (Now very slow, heavy and ominous) But see.... the king comes here, Kreon.... the son of Menoikeus whom the gods have appointed for us.... in our recent change of fortune. What matter is it, I wonder, that leads him to call us together?

Antigone chorus 2

Peter Patterson

Moderate and unhurried, but fast enough to keep the dance quality

This famous chorus is not sung but spoken rhythmically to the flute's accompaniment. Each bar of the flute's melody must fit each line of the poem. The player and speakers must be very attentive to one another to keep in time, the flute often pausing slightly at the end of bars to fit exactly to the beginning of the chorus's next line. On the other hand, the flute player will sometimes shorten the rest at the end of the melody to begin the next verse with the speakers.

1. Many the wonders yet none
   so great as the wonder of man.
   Over the ocean gray
   with the winds of the south he will sail,
   plunging through perilous deeps.

2. Earth, the immortal, of gods
   is greatest and tireless still,
   yet with his horse and plough
   year after year man travails,
   turning the soil to his will.

3. Cunning, he masters the beasts
   and snares the swift birds of the wild,
   harvests the fish from the deeps
   and tames the richly maned horses,
   yoking the wild mountain bulls.

4. Speech he has learned, and thought
   that moves with the speed of the wind;
   living in cities, he learns
   to order a well founded state,
   safe from the frost and the rain.

5. Never is man at a loss,
   resourceful at every new turn;
   death is the only foe
   against whom no cure can be found,
   though he may master disease.

6. Passing belief are the skills
   and arts of mankind, though his knowledge
   leads to both good and to ill.
   Homeless the evil man stays,
   never my hearth shall he share.

Antigone chorus 3

WARNING: C flat indicates a quarter tone half way between C and B natural

Peter Patterson

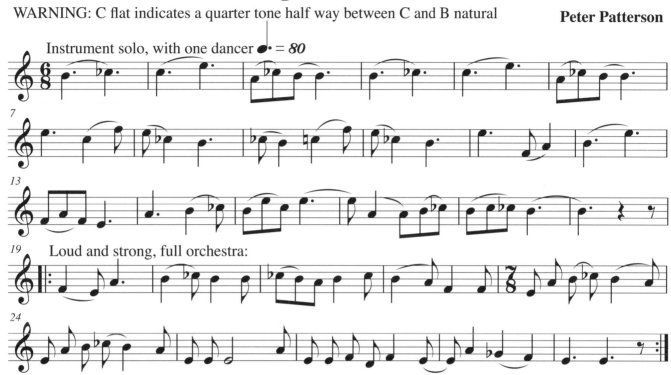

All my choruses from Antigone are in forms of the Dorian mode, which in Ancient Greece was from our keyboard E to E on the white notes (unlike the Middle Ages Dorian which was from D to D). Each Greek scale had three basic forms: diatonic, chromatic, enharmonic. This accompaniment is in the enharmonic form, which uses very expressive quarter notes (half of a semi-tone). If you are using a harp or lyre you must retune it for this piece. If a recorder with Baroque fingering is playing, you need to finger C half-flat from the top as open closed open closed closed closed open, and thumb on. The C in bar two is a normal C natural.

The first 18 bars are best just played on one instrument, lyre or woodwind, very expressive, with one able dancer performing alone. The rest of the chorus dancers stand and watch. At the repeat bar as many instruments as possible join in. It is a strong, assertive dance with strong foot movements. A competent conductor is needed in rehearsals to keep the speaking chorus (words overleaf) in time with the orchestra. The choreographer needs to understand that the four stanzas represent Strophe Alpha, Antistrophe Alpha, Strophe Beta, Antistrophe Beta, on alternate sides of the stage.

Continued over....   121

Peter Patterson

In Chorus 3 percussion instruments, such as hand drums and tambourine, should only enter in the second section, "loud and strong, full orchestra". In all the choruses the percussion should be used only to emphasize the metre, so basically that means a good thump at the beginning of each bar. In this chorus, though, there could be more, as I have suggested above, to support the swaying movement in the music, even with the occasional lead-in of sixteenths (semi-quavers) as shown. The percussion players need to learn to support the metre changes, not make trouble for them!

In the four stanzas, or strophes, the first two can be recited with the solo intrument in the background, or - if that is too difficult to get properly together - recite those stanzas without accompaniment after the solo, then using the "loud and strong" music to support the third and fourth stanzas. The speakers must be loud and strong, too, and very clear, so as to be easily understood. Here are the words in my metric translation:

1. (strophe alpha) How happy they who do not know the taste of evil!
   From / any house that heaven's wrath but once has shaken
   Never will the woe and suffering depart
   But cling to every generation / weighing down the dreadful debt
   With / all the ocean's power / when the dark storm drives
   The / black sand from the water's deeps, / when the Thracian gales roar,
   Booming on the angry wind / up the wild, desolate shore.

2. (antistrophe) From olden times the house of Labdakos is stricken,
   Since no atonement has been found the curse lives on;
   Down each one is flung until the wrathful god
   His will has wrought, for no salvation / ever can redeem their fate.
   But now the thick red dust / is strewn on the tree's last root:
   It smothers the last faint root of promise / which Oedipus' house had left,
   Crushing out the pride of heart, sin of a presumptuous tongue.

3. (strophe beta) No man's pride can match your power,
   O Zeus, beyond both sleep and time,
   Who lives in bright Olympus
   Now and ever more.
   The ancient law must always hold:
   Never a gift to mortal man without its shadowy side!

4. (antistrophe) True enough that hope can raise
   A man and comfort him in life,
   But many, too, it tricks
   And lures to his doom.
   The saying holds: The fated man,
   Sensing the pain of his predestined fall, will turn to evil!

Antigone chorus 4

Peter Patterson
(music and text translation)

Dance rhythms, not too fast, up to ♩ = *120*

O love that in bat-tle can-not be con-quered, love, that des-troys and ru-ins— wealth, that

keeps sleep a-way from ev-'ry man's door and makes him de-sire a soft girl's— cheeks, that

fol-lows him e-ver o-ver the sea and in-to the hum-blest coun-try— place:

No— god can es-cape it, nor a-ny mor-tal man.—

Instruments

The

sligh-test car-ress of love seiz-es a-ny one with— mad-ness!

2. The just mind you drag away from its course,
   injustice, dishonour, then is its lot.
   The brothers, both men of one father's blood,
   you stirred with desire and madness to fight.
   The conqueror none can be but desire,
   inflamed by the lovely sight of a bride.
   Sharing the throne is desire, wielding the sceptre of law....
   and none can defeat the goddess who mocks us: Aphrodite!

The sentiments in all the Antigone choruses are very male oriented. Sophocles was aware of that and, not surprisingly, the chorus here consists of a group of grumpy old men. In the first verse, the "strophe alpha", they again dance on one side of the stage, then gyrate to the other side for the second verse, the "antistrophe alpha". Ancient Greek plays were musicals with lots of dancing.

In addition to the unaccustomed scale in this dance (E F G-flat A-natural B C D E) the rhythms will be new to most western students, too. In the ancient world, dance rhythms were mostly asymetric or compound, based on fives, sevens, elevens, and so on. In many countries they still are - for example, Turkey, Bulgaria, Ladakh and other Himalayan regions. In the European Middle Ages, dances were in three-time, fours were banned by the Church as leading too deep into matter. Virtually all popular western music is now in fours!

Antigone chorus 5

Peter Patterson

This dance should be supported by a tambourine playing long-short-short (quarter-eighth-eighth) throughout, stopping only to pause together with the music at the end of each strophe. This chorus is also spoken, in time with the melody, not sung. A good conductor is again essential to attain precision. The music can be played (and danced to) between the strophes without the chorus to give more attention to the choreography - and to give the speakers a break!

1. Such was the fate of fair Danae (note: pronounce Da-na-e, three syllables),
   Locked in her brazen bower
   Far from the solace of sunlight,
   Yet on that noblest of maidens
   Fell from the father on high
   A wonderful gleaming shower
   Of life-giving grace. Such is fate that
   No / strongly-built ship on the angry sea
   Ever can stay her power.

2. Thus, too, imprisoned in stone,
   The haughty Edonian king
   Was pent at Dionysos' bidding (pronounce Dee-on-ee-sos, accent on the 'on')
   Till, all his passion full spent,
   Right understanding had dawned
   As to which god his tongue had offended
   When he had striven to shatter
   The fiery spell of the Maenads -
   Wild, yes, but sacred their revels,
   Dancing with song in the hills.

Antigone chorus 6: final

Peter Patterson

Continued over....

Antigone chorus & percussion

Peter Patterson

Midsummer Music

Peter Patterson

The rich harmonies of this round are appreciated by Class 6 upwards.

The words are an adaptation of a verse by Herbert Hahn.

Winter

Peter Patterson

Win - ter's chill now binds the land with its bit - ter thong.

Far lie sweet sum - mer's joys, the dark will last yet long.

Sad - ly my heart longs for the mer - ry black - bird's song.

In this wistful three-part round I wanted to capture the flavour of the late Middle Ages, with its music's parallel fifths and, to our ears, strange harmonic cadences. It could be sung when the students study the Middle Ages or early Renaissance.

The Forest Folk

Peter Patterson

Moderate speed, relaxed

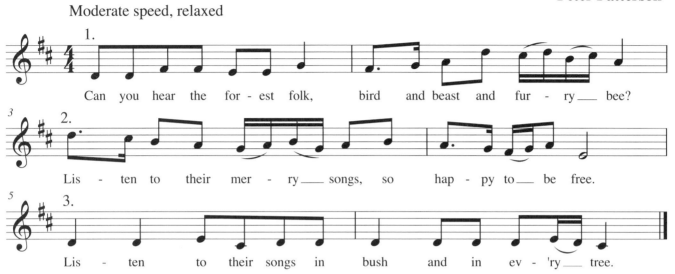

1. Can you hear the for-est folk, bird and beast and fur - ry ___ bee?

2. Lis - ten to their mer - ry ___ songs, so hap - py to ___ be free.

3. Lis - ten to their songs in bush and in ev - 'ry ___ tree.

This is a simple round which could be sung in Class 4 or 5. Stop on 'bee', 'free' and 'tree'.

Koko, the Clown

Peter Patterson

Ko - ko, the clown, and me are friends, he jug - gles and rides the tight - rope wire,

ri - ding a bike with just one wheel and brea - thing out clouds of fire.

This little tune is a two-part canon, with the two parts coming in quite close together. It can be sung through several times, each part repeating without a pause or slowing down; and when it finishes, each part must be sung to the end, not finishing together as we do in a round. It's trickier to write than a round and trickier to sing, too.

Magic Bee Song

Peter Patterson

Not too fast

The past you had for-got-ten is grow-ing ev-'ry day, through cast-les wrought of sil-ver-stone and their dra-gon schools at play, to the gree-ning of the gol-den age and the young sun's rain-bow land, to the vales the elves still call their own where fire moun-tains stand. Ride with the Elf Queen out on the breeze; dance with a ma-gic swarm of bees! Oh come with me! Oh come with me!

2. In the / mountains there are serpent paths still hidden from your sight,
but even the fierce giant kings know dawn must end the night.
The spirit of the rising sun, that is your oldest friend
has come again to stroke your eyes and make the long night end.
Ride with the Elf Queen out on the breeze,
dance with a magic swarm of bees!
Oh come with me! Come with me!

This is a song for the older students (from my novel, "Fal") and can be sung to the guitar chords shown, or you can score the chords for whatever instruments you have available. Use the lettered guitar chords as the bass line if you do that.

Beethoven's Impatience

Beethoven/Patterson

Very moderate, strong and confident

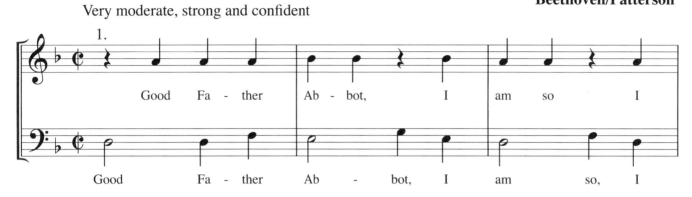

Good Fa – ther Ab – bot, I am so I

Good Fa – ther Ab – bot, I am so, I

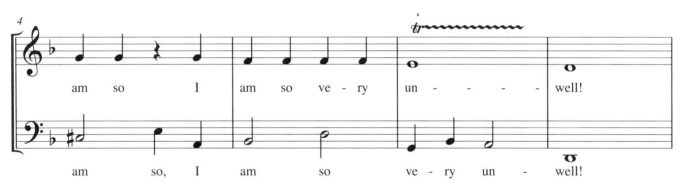

am so I am so ve – ry un – – – well!

am so, I am so ve – ry un – well!

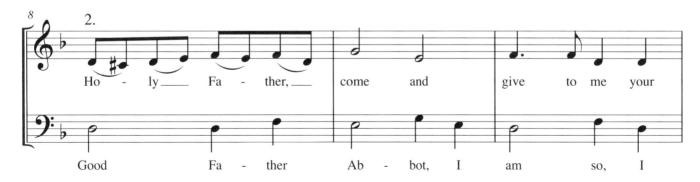

Ho – ly Fa – ther, come and give to me your

Good Fa – ther Ab – bot, I am so, I

136

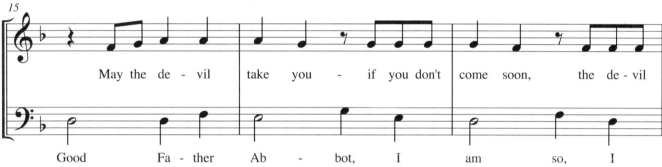

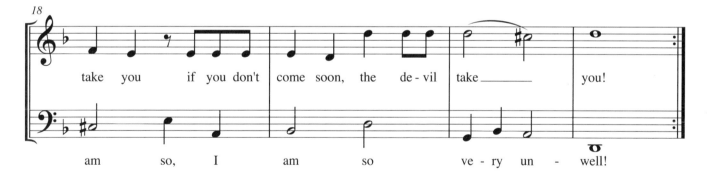

This is a very popular round with older students. I have translated Beethoven's humorous words and added a bass-line for the cello - or you could get someone with a deep voice to sing it to the first 7 bars of the words.

Climbing Up

Peter Patterson

This is a simple warming up exercise at the beginning of a singing session, for the class or for the choir. Often we just use scales to do this - one key higher on every repetition. Isn't that a rather dull way to begin, though?

This exercise is just a little more fun and the words might raise a smile here and there, too. Start lower than C if you want, and go as high as the singers are able, but keep the breathing relaxed and deep - and avoid stress at all times.

Peace Song

Peter Patterson

With vigour

Let it sound from all the peo - ples of the world: Work for friend - ship! Let the ban - ner be un - furled and we'll all live in peace with each and ev' - ry one.

This Peace Song can be sung as a round or in unison. There are two more verses:

2. Understanding is the road that we must run,
   Work for friendship!
   Then the victory can be won,
   and we'll all live in peace with each and ev'ryone.

3. Hear the cry from all who live beneath the sun:
   Work for friendship!
   It's the task no one may shun,
   till we all live in peace with each and ev'ryone.

Salve Regina I

Peter Patterson

This is a two-part round suitable for Class 7 and above. Very simple, in which the students should concentrate on singing in tune so that the intervals between the parts consist of really true and pure thirds, and so on. Be careful that no one hurries the eighth-notes in bars 3 and 7 but listens to the other part to get the notes clearly coinciding.

Salve Regina 2

Peter Patterson

Slow and full sounding ♩ = 80

Sal - - ve, Re - gi - - - na,
ma - ter mi - se - ri - cor - - di - ae,
vi - ta dul - ce - - - do _____
et spes nos - tra, sal - - - ve! _____

This is a four-part round with rich harmonies. Because of the four voices even more attention must be given to listening to the intervals and harmonies than in Salve Regina 1 to get the intonation just right and to produce really resonant chords.

Seasons

Peter Patterson

Moderate speed

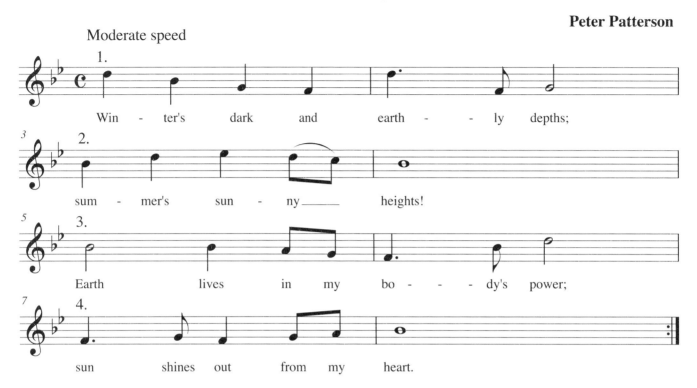

Win - ter's dark and earth - - ly depths;

sum - mer's sun - ny heights!

Earth lives in my bo - - - dy's power;

sun shines out from my heart.

Shadow World

Peter Patterson

Continued over....

I've a sha-dow too, I'll share the fact with you. Want to draw that

I've a sha - dow, see my sha - dow, Want to draw?

sha - dow? Just as you had feared, it's se - ri - ous - ly weird and to

Yes, I'll draw. Sure, I feared it, weird and feared to

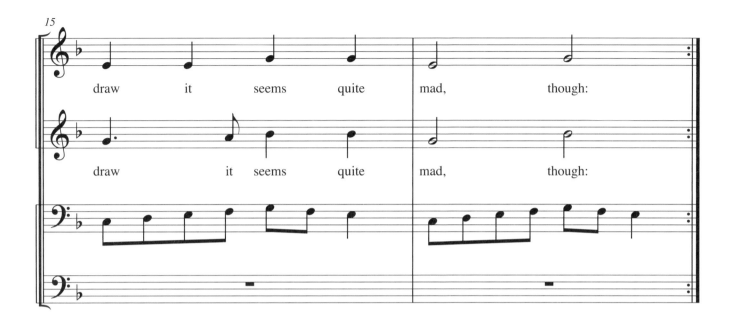

In Classes 7 and 8, when the students are 12 to 14 years old, they will be learning to construct shadows in perspective drawing and to draw from observation, beginning with simple geometrical objects like spheres and cones, drawing these forms together with their shadows.

If you use a double bass in the accompaniment to this song and a student finds the part I have suggested too difficult, just play D and C in two bars each using half notes (minims).

When you come to the repeat bar go straight back to the beginning, go round and round as often as you like. The music should stop suddenly, with no run on, anywhere that the conductor chooses, different each time. Good practice for the students to learn to follow the conductor!

Dragon Dances

For baby and mature dragons

Peter Patterson

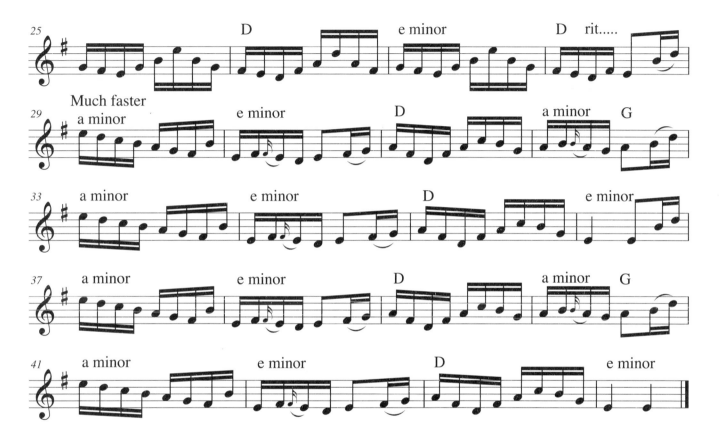

Each of the sections could be repeated before entering the next section if you want to make the whole dance longer. Actually, dragons like that!

Dragon Dances

For elegant dragons

Peter Patterson

Continued over....

Summer's End

Peter Patterson

This is a simple two-part round which can be sung with or without the accompaniment suggested.
And don't be bound by the instruments I have specified; use whatever you have.

The Birch Tree and the Wild Rose

Peter Patterson

Lord Tho-mas and his Fair — An-net — sat — all day on — a hill; — When —

night was come, — and sun — was set — they had not talked their — fill. — Lord

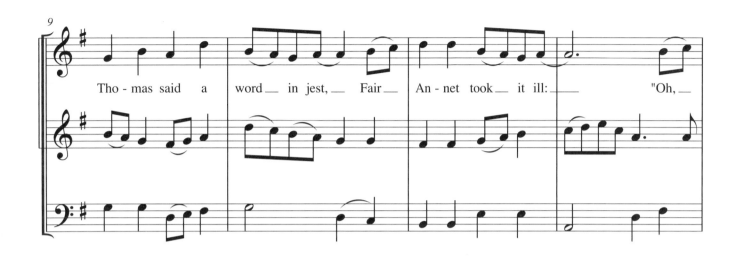

Tho - mas said a word — in jest, — Fair — An - net took — it ill: — "Oh,

I will ne - ver wed — a wife — a - gainst my own friends' — will." — "If

Continued over....

After every group of three verses the violin and cello (or whatever instruments you have) play their first eight bars without the singer(s) as an interlude.

4. "Oh speak, oh speak, dear mother," he says, "a good word speak to me.
   Oh shall I take the nut-brown bride and let Fair Annet be?"

5. "The nut-brown bride has gold and gear, Fair Annet she has none,
   And the little beauty Fair Annet has, oh it will soon be gone."

6. "Yes, I will take my mother's advice and marry me out of hand,
   And I will take the nut-brown bride. Fair Annet may leave the land."

7. The horse Fair Annet rode upon, he ambled like the wind,
   With silver he was shod before, with burning gold behind.

8. And four and twenty silver bells were all tied to his mane,
   And every gust of the northland wind, they tinkled one by one.

9. And when she came into the church, she shimmered like the sun;
   The belt that was about her waist was all with pearls bedone.

10. She sat her by the nut-brown bride, and her eyes they were so clear,
    Lord Thomas clean forgot the bride when Fair Annet drew near.

11. He took a rose into his hand, he gave it kisses three,
    And reaching by the nut-brown bride, laid it on Fair Annet's knee.

12. The nut-brown bride she up and spoke, she spoke with mickle spite,
    "And where got ye that rose water that makes your skin so white?"

13. The bride she drew a bobkin long from out her gay head-gear
    And struck Fair Annet into the heart that word spake never more.

14. Lord Thomas saw Annet wax pale and marvelled what might be,
    But when he saw her dear heart's blood all wood-wrath waxéd he.

15. He drew his dirk that was so sharp, that was so sharp and meet,
    And drae it into the nut-brown bride that fell down dead at his feet.

16. "Now stay for me, dear Annet," he said, "now stay for me!" he cried
    Then struck the dagger into his heart and fell dead by his side.

17. Lord Thomas lies without kirk wall, Fair Annet within the choir,
    And o'er the one there grew a birch, the other a bonny briar.

Traditional ballad

The Chevy Chase

Peter Patterson

hound and horn Earl Per-cy took __ the way: __ the child may rue __ that is un-born the

hun-ting of __ that day! __

[Fiddle]

Continued over....

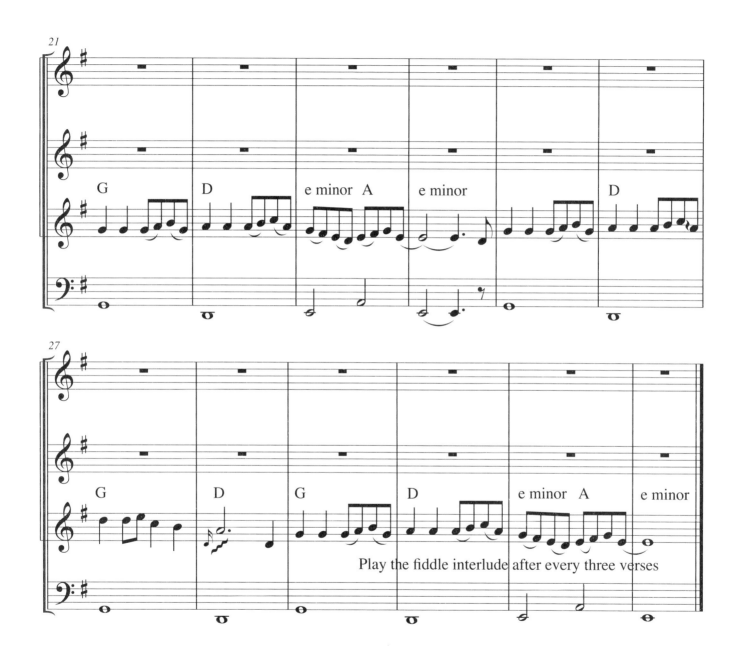

Play the fiddle interlude after every three verses

158

2. The stout Earl of Northumberland a vow to God did make
   his pleasure in the Scottish woods three summer's days to take
   the chiefest harts in Chevy Chase to kill and bear away:
   These tidings to Earl Douglas came in Scotland where he lay.

3. The gallant greyhounds swiftly ran to chase the fallow deer;
   On Monday they began to hunt 'ere daylight did appear;
   And long before high noon they had a hundred fat bucks slain -
   then, having dined, the drovers went to rouse the deer again.

4. Lo, yonder doth Earl Douglas come, his men in armour bright;
   Full twenty hundred Scottish spears all marching in our sight.
   "All men of pleasant Tivydale, fast by the River Tweede,
   Oh cease your sports!" Earl Percy said, "and take your bows with speed!"

5. Earl Douglas on his milk white steed, most like a baron bold,
   rode foremost of his company, whose armour shone like gold.
   "Show me," said he, "whose men ye be that hunt so boldly here,
   that without my consent do chase and kill my fallow deer!"

6. Our English archers bent their bows, their hearts were good and true;
   At the first flight of arrows sent full four score Scots they slew.
   Oh Christ! it was great grief to see how each man chose his spear
   and how the blood out of their breasts did gush like water clear.

7. At last these two stout earls did meet, like captains of great might,
   like lions wood they layed on lode (= like angry lions they fought), they made a cruel fight.
   They fought until they both did sweat, with swords of tempered steel,
   till blood all down their cheeks like rain they trickling down did feel.

8. With that there came an arrow keen out of an English bow
   which struck Earl Douglas on the breast a deep and deadly blow.
   A knight amongst the Scots there was that saw Earl Douglas die,
   who straight in heart did vow vengeance upon the Lord Percy.

9. And past the English archers all, without all dread and fear,
   and through Earl Percy's body then he thrust his hateful spear.
   Of fifteen hundred Englishmen went home but fifty three;
   The rest in Chevy Chase were slain, under the greenwood tree.

Fiddle Dance

Peter Patterson

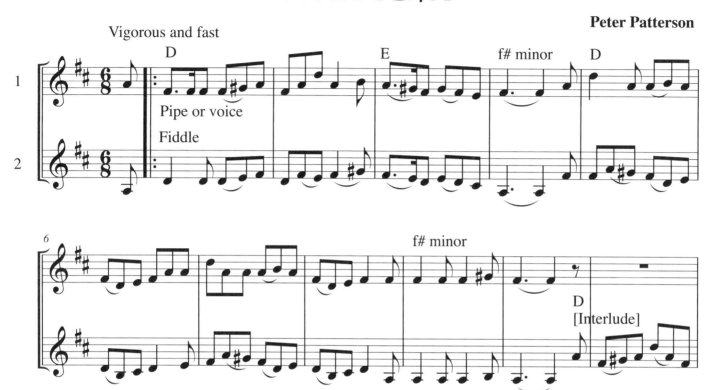

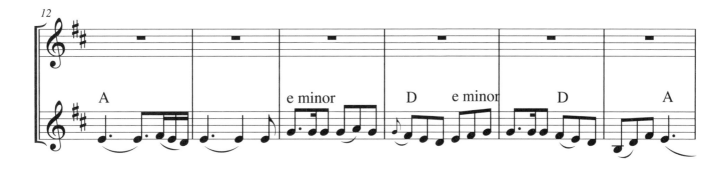

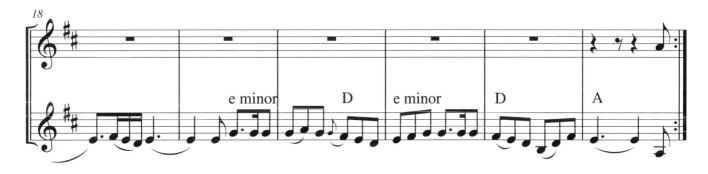

This is a fun piece for pipe(s) and a fiddle and goes wonderfully to Frodo's disastrous song at The Prancing Pony. It has been a favourite for many years with Classes 4 and 5 but was also the only song that could stop my son crying when he was 9 months old! He listened to the many verses with a wide smile.

Notice that in the Interlude for fiddle the G# has become G natural.

The Rainbow

Peter Patterson

162

Continued over....

air   has   a   doub - le rain - bow   there! _____

rain - bows   are   love - ly   things,   look, there's   a   rain - bow   now!

rain - bows   are   love - ly   things,   look, there's   a   rain - bow   now!

rain - bows   are   love - ly   things,   so   love - ly!

Ah! _____

Ah! _____

Ah! _____

The Rainbow

Second verse

Peter Patterson

Again, four bars introduction from the ostinato singers

See

how that love - ly rain - bow __ throws her jew - elled __ arm a -

round this world __ when the rain goes! And __ how I wish the

rain would __ come __ a - gain __ and a gain! _____

The poem is by W. H. Davies

Yr Hen Wr Mwyn - The Kind Old Man

Welsh trad., edited Patterson

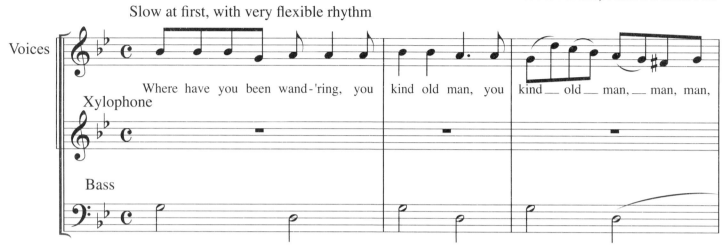

Slow at first, with very flexible rhythm

Where have you been wand-'ring, you kind old man, you kind __ old __ man, __ man, man,

man, man, man, the __ kind-est soul a - live? Out for some fish-ing, boys,

fal - dee ree - dee rye - doh,   fal - dee ree - dee ree - dle oh,   fal - dee ree - dee rye - doh!

Two players

2. What fish what you catching, you kind old man (et cetera....)
   Flat-fish, a couple, boys, faldee reedee ryedoh (et cetera....)

3. Your clothes had a wetting, and how, old man, you kind....
   Falling in the river, boys, faldee reedee....

4. But why do you shiver, you kind old man, you kind....
   Cold from the wetting, boys, faldee reedee....

5. But if it should end you, what then, old man, you kind....
   Then I'll be buried, boys, faldee reedee....

6. Where would you be buried, you kind old man, you kind....
   Under the hearth stone, boys, faldee reedee....

7. Why under the hearth stone, you kind old man, you kind....
   To hear the porridge bubbling, boys, faldee reedee....

Song list on accompanying CD

1	Introduction by Peter Patterson	36	Now the day has come
2	My Pigeon House	37	The Golden Time
3	Mother of the Fairy Tale	38	Coffee Song
4	Golden Sun, Arise	39	Flying Song
5	Little Mary Winecups	40	Acrobat
6	Good Angel	41	Joyous is the Day
7	The Heavens Above	42	Pretty Colours
8	The Lady Moon	43	Song of the Nature Spirits
9	The Water of Life	44	Song of the Nature Spirits 2
10	The Sun is in my Heart	45	Birds
11	Easy Questions	46	Vedic chant – to Vishnu
12	King Mansolain	47	Gayatri Mantra
13	King Mansolain 2	48	Egyptian Dance
14	King Mansolain 3	49	Hymn to U-si-re
15	The King of the Copper Mountains	50	Gilgamesh
16	Granny's Wonderful Chair	51	Searching Satyrs 1
17	Painting Song	52	Searching Satyrs 3
18	The King of Ireland's Son 1	53	Searching Satyrs 2
19	The King of Ireland's Son 2	54	Merry Let Us Be
20	The King of Ireland's Son 4	55	Swallows
21	Number Song	56	The Elven Halleluia
22	Ring Dance for the Lord	57	Michael, the Victorious
23	Ring Dance 2	58	Michael Song 2
24	Solomon's Temple	59	Michael Song 3
25	I Greet the Day	60	Bulgarian Dance Rhythms
26	Of All Created Things	61	Music from West Africa
27	Odin, the Wanderer	62	West Africa 2: Evua, the Sun God
28	Music for a Norse Play 1	63	Antigone chorus 1
29	Norse Play 2	64	Antigone chorus 4
30	Poetic Edda	65	Antigone chorus 6
31	Sigurd and the Dragon	66	Midsummer Music
32	Snow White	67	Winter: round
33	Celtic Blessing	68	The Forest Folk
34	The Lord of Falkenstein	69	Koko, the Clown
35	Kalevala	70	Summer's End